Essential Test Tips Video from Trivium Test Prep

Dear Customer,

Thank you for purchasing from Trivium Test Prep! Whether you're looking to join the military, get into college, or advance your career, we're honored to be a part of your journey.

To show our appreciation (and to help you relieve a little of that test-prep stress), we're offering a **FREE *CNA Essential Test Tips* Video** by Trivium Test Prep. Our video includes 35 test preparation strategies that will help keep you calm and collected before and during your big exam. All we ask is that you email us your feedback and describe your experience with our product. Amazing, awful, or just so-so: we want to hear what you have to say!

To receive your **FREE *CNA Essential Test Tips* Video**, please email us at 5star@triviumtestprep.com. Include "Free 5 Star" in the subject line and the following information in your email:

1. The title of the product you purchased.
2. Your rating from 1 – 5 (with 5 being the best).
3. Your feedback about the product, including how our materials helped you meet your goals and ways in which we can improve our products.
4. Your full name and shipping address so we can send your **FREE *CNA Essential Test Tips* Video**.

If you have any questions or concerns please feel free to contact us directly at 5star@triviumtestprep.com.

Thank you, and good luck with your studies!

CNA Study Guide 2024-2025

7 Practice Tests and Prep Book for the
Certified Nursing Assistant Exam [6th Edition]

Jeremy Downs

Copyright ©2024 Trivium Test Prep

ISBN-13: 9781637989852

ALL RIGHTS RESERVED. By purchase of this book, you have been licensed on copy for personal use only. No part of this work may be reproduced, redistributed, or used in any form or by any means without prior written permission of the publisher and copyright owner. Trivium Test Prep; Accepted, Inc.; Cirrus Test Prep; and Ascencia Test Prep are all imprints of Trivium Test Prep, LLC.

The National Council of State Boards of Nursing, Inc. was not involved in the creation or production of this product, is not in any way affiliated with Ascencia Test Prep, and does not sponsor or endorse this product.

TABLE OF CONTENTS

Introduction 1
    The Certification Process 2
    The Written/Oral Exam 2
    The Skills Evaluation 3
    NNAAP Skills List for Skills Evaluation 3
    Exam Administration 4

Activities of Daily Living 6
    Hygiene 6
    Dressing and Grooming 11
    Nutrition and Hydration 14
    Elimination 18
    Patient Comfort and Safety 22
    Fall Prevention 23
    Lifting, Transferring, and Positioning Patients 24

Basic Nursing Skills 31
    Vital Signs 34
    Specimen Collection and Testing 40
    Wounds 42
    Restraints 43

Safety and Infection Control 46
    Infection Control 46
    Emergency Response 53
    Fire and Electrical Safety 58

Psychosocial Care Skills 61
    Emotional, Spiritual, and Cultural Needs 61
    Mental Health Needs 62

Role of the Nurse Aide 65
    Client Rights 67
    Legal and Ethical Behavior 68

Members of the Health Care Team 69
Practice Test #1 .... **73**
Answer Explanations #1 .... **83**
Practice Test #2 .... **91**
Answer Explanations #2 .... **102**
Practice Test #3 .... **110**
Answer Explanations #3 .... **120**
Practice Test #4 .... **127**
Answer Explanations #4 .... **135**

ONLINE RESOURCES

Ascencia includes online resources with the purchase of this study guide to help you fully prepare for the exam.

Practice Tests

In addition to the four practice exams included in this book, we also offer three exams online. Since many exams today are computer based, practicing your test-taking skills on the computer is a great way to prepare.

Review Questions

Need more practice? Our review questions use a variety of formats to help you memorize key terms and concepts.

Flash Cards

Trivium's flash cards allow you to review important terms easily on your computer or smartphone.

Cheat Sheets

Review the core skills you need to master the exam with easy-to-read Cheat Sheets.

From Stress to Success

Watch "From Stress to Success," a brief but insightful YouTube video that offers the tips, tricks, and secrets experts use to score higher on the exam.

Reviews

Leave a review, send us helpful feedback, or sign up for Trivium promotions—including free books!

Access these materials by following the link or scanning the QR code:

ascenciatestprep.com/cna-online-resources

Introduction

Congratulations on choosing to take the Certified Nurse Assistant/Aide (CNA) exam! Passing the CNA exam is an important step forward in your health care career, and we're here to help you feel prepared on exam day.

The certification process for nurse assistants/aides varies from state to state. The information in this introduction will cover the details of the National Nurse Aide Assessment Program (NNAAP) exam, which is used in the following states and territories:

- Alabama
- New Hampshire
- Alaska
- North Carolina
- California
- Colorado
- Pennsylvania
- Rhode Island
- Washington
- District of Columbia
- South Carolina
- Maryland
- Georgia
- Texas
- Mississippi
- Virginia
- Virgin Islands
- Minnesota

If your state or territory doesn't use the NNAAP exam, don't worry! The concepts and practice questions in this book can still help you prepare for your state's exam. Check with your state's Nurse Aide Registry to find out how to become certified in your state.

The Certification Process

The National Nurse Aide Assessment Program (NNAAP) exam includes a written exam and practical skills evaluation. To qualify for the exams, candidates must have completed a state-approved nurse assistant/aide training course within the previous two years. Some states will also allow candidates with other training (e.g., licensed nurse coursework) to qualify for certification. The exam is given at Pearson VUE testing centers, and applications for the exam are completed on the Pearson VUE website. You can visit the NNAAP website at https://www.ncsbn.org/nnaap-and-mace.htm to find the application for your state.

The Written/Oral Exam

The written exam consists of 70 multiple-choice questions. Ten of these questions are unscored: they are included on the exam so the test makers can try out new questions. You will have two hours to complete the exam.

Candidates who have difficulty reading English may take the multiple-choice exam in an oral format. Some states also offer a Spanish language version of the oral exam. The candidate will be able to listen to the questions and will then mark the correct answer in the test booklet. The oral form of the test includes the same number of questions as the written form.

The written/oral exam covers three content areas that test the candidate's knowledge of terms, concepts, and skills relevant to being a nurse assistant/aide.

CNA Exam Content		
Content Area	**Detailed Content**	**Number of Scored Questions**
I. Physical Care Skills	Activities of Daily Living • hygiene • dressing and grooming • nutrition and hydration • elimination • rest/sleep/comfort	9
	Basic Nursing Skills • infection control • safety/emergency • therapeutic and technical procedures • data collection and reporting	23
	Restorative Skills • prevention • self care/independence	5

CNA Exam Content

Content Area	Detailed Content	Number of Scored Questions
II. Psychosocial Care Skills	Emotional and Mental Health Needs	6
	Spiritual and Cultural Needs	2
III. Role of the Nurse Aide	Communication	4
	Client Rights	4
	Legal and Ethical Behavior	2
	Member of the Health Care Team	5
Total		**60**

The Skills Evaluation

The skills evaluation is a practical, hands-on exam that requires candidates to perform nurse assistant/aide skills. The skills will be demonstrated on a simulated patient using real equipment. A Nurse Assistant Evaluator will compare your performance to the required steps listed in the NNAAP Skills List.

The NNAAP list includes 22 tested skills. You will be asked to perform **FIVE** of these skills. Some states have a skill that is always included on the exam (e.g., handwashing), but this varies by state.

NNAAP Skills List for Skills Evaluation

Skill 1: Hand Hygiene (Hand Washing)

Skill 2: Applies One Knee-High Elastic Stocking

Skill 3: Assists to Ambulate Using Transfer Belt

Skill 4: Assists with Use of Bedpan

Skill 5: Cleans Upper or Lower Denture

Skill 6: Counts and Records Radial Pulse

Skill 7: Counts and Records Respirations

Skill 8: Donning and Removing PPE (Gown and Gloves) Skill 9: Dresses Client with Affected (Weak) Right Arm Skill 10: Feeds Client Who Cannot Feed Self

Skill 11: Gives Modified Bed Bath (Face and One Arm, Hand and Underarm)

Skill 12: Measures and Records Electronic Blood Pressure Skill 13: Measures and Records Urinary Output

Skill 14: Measures and Records Weight of Ambulatory Client

Skill 15: Performs Modified Passive Range of Motion (PROM) for One Knee and One Ankle

Skill 16: Performs Modified Passive Range of Motion (PROM) for One Shoulder

Skill 17: Positions on Side

Skill 18: Provides Catheter Care for Female

Skill 19: Provides Foot Care on One Foot

Skill 20: Provides Mouth Care

Skill 21: Provides Perineal Care (Peri-Care) for Female Skill 22: Transfers from Bed to Wheelchair Using Transfer Belt

Skill 23: Measures and Records Manual Blood Pressure

*Skill 12: Measures and Records Electronic Blood Pressure is no longer tested.

In this study guide, we have included all the skills in special boxes alongside the relevant study content. These boxes provide simplified, step-by-step instructions for each skill. Steps in bold are **critical element steps**: if these steps are not completed correctly, you will fail that skill. For the complete list of skills, visit the Pearson VUE website.

Exam Administration

To register for the exam, you must first apply through the Pearson VUE website (https://home.pearsonvue.com/testtaker). You will be asked to submit the necessary documents to prove that you meet the eligibility requirements. Once the appropriate state agency has approved your application, you will be scheduled to take the exam.

The exam is offered at Pearson VUE testing centers. You will have three months from the acceptance of your application to take the exam. If you do not take the exam within the three-month window, you will have to resubmit your application.

Plan to arrive at least 30 minutes before the exam to complete biometric screening. You will need two forms of government-issued ID. Be prepared to be photographed and have your palm scanned. Your primary ID must be government issued, include a recent photograph and signature, and match the name under which you registered to take the test. If you do not have proper ID, you will not be allowed to take the test.

You will not be allowed to bring study material or electronic devices, including phones, programmable calculators, or smart watches, into the testing room. The testing site will provide lockers for valuables.

Exam Results

How you receive your results will depend on the state you test in. Some states deliver results on the same day as the test. In other states, you will receive your results through your Pearson VUE account after several days.

If you fail either the written/oral exam or the skills evaluation, you will be able to retake the exam. In most states, you will have three chances to take the exam. If you fail three times, you will have to retake a nursing assistant/aide training course.

Using This Book

This book is divided into two sections. In the content area review, you will find a summary of the knowledge and skills included in the exam content outline. Throughout the chapter you'll also see Quick Review Questions that will help reinforce important concepts and skills.

The book also includes two full-length practice tests (one in the book and one online) with answer rationales. You can use these tests to gauge your readiness for the test and determine which content areas you may need to review more thoroughly.

Ascencia Test Prep

With health care fields such as nursing, pharmacy, emergency care, and physical therapy becoming the fastest-growing industries in the United States, individuals looking to enter the health care industry or rise in their field need high- quality, reliable resources. Ascencia Test Prep's study guides and test preparation materials are developed by credentialed industry professionals with years of experience in their respective fields. Ascencia recognizes that health care professionals nurture bodies and spirits, and save lives. Ascencia Test Prep's mission is to help health care workers grow.

Activities of Daily Living

Hygiene

Oral Care

Oral care prevents tooth decay and odors and promotes comfort. Many different medical conditions can cause oral problems. However, every patient, regardless of diagnosis, requires oral care. Equipment for providing oral care includes a towel, facecloth, paper towels, gloves, toothpaste, toothbrush, toothette (swab), floss, cup of water, kidney basin, and mouthwash.

Flossing should be done after brushing the patient's teeth. When preparing to floss a patient's teeth, first ensure that flossing is not contraindicated. To start, break off a piece of floss, and move it gently up and down between teeth. Start at the back of the right side of the mouth and work around to the left side.

> **HELPFUL HINT**
> For the skills evaluation:
> - Start the skill by explaining the procedure to the patient and closing the curtain for privacy.
> - End each skill by disposing of gloves and washing hands.

> **HELPFUL HINT**
> Always watch for signs of choking when providing mouth care.

Denture care includes the cleaning and proper storage of patient dentures. The nurse aide may need to remove the dentures from the patient's mouth by grasping them lightly with a piece of gauze. Once clean, place dentures in a cup labeled with the patient's name and other necessary information (e.g., room number).

Skills Evaluation: Clean Upper or Lower Denture

1. Wash hands and put on gloves.
2. Line sink with a towel.
3. Rinse dentures under lukewarm water.
4. Brush dentures with soft brush and denture paste.
5. Rinse dentures and denture cup.
6. Place dentures in denture cup half-filled with water or solution.
7. Dispose of towel and rinse toothbrush.
8. Remove gloves and wash hands.

> **HELPFUL HINT**
> Never use hot water or regular toothpaste on dentures.

When providing oral care for unconscious patients, treat the patient as if they were conscious (i.e., identify yourself and explain the task). If not contraindicated, raise the bed to 30 degrees and position the patient close to the side of the bed before starting.

> **HELPFUL HINT**
> Avoid triggering the gag reflex when swabbing the tongue and roof of mouth.

Once the patient is positioned, place a towel under the patient's head and a basin beneath their chin. Apply water-soluble lubricant to the patient's lips, and gently separate the patient's jaw with a padded tongue depressor. (Never force the teeth apart.)

Wet a toothette with the prescribed solution or mouthwash. Squeeze out excess solution and thoroughly swab the mouth from top to bottom.

When cleaning is finished, use chlorhexidine mouthwash or water to rinse the toothettes. Change toothette as needed.

Quick Review Question

1. After cleaning dentures, the nurse aide should place the clean dentures:
    A) on a clean, dry towel next to the sink.
    B) in a cup of water on the patient's bedside.
    C) back in the patient's mouth.
    D) in the appropriate trash receptacle.

Bathing

Bathing can help a patient feel better, improve circulation, prevent odors and infection, and provide an opportunity to spot an injury. Follow the physician's orders and the patient's preferences regarding when and how often the patient should bathe and what cleansers to use.

Equipment includes gloves, at least two towels, five to six washcloths, bath blankets, bed linen to change the patient's bedding, a wash basin with warm water, skin cleanser, skin lotion or skin barrier cream, and clean clothing.

Bed baths are given to patients who cannot bathe in a tub or shower. Start with the face, then move to the arms, chest, legs, and feet. Place a towel under each limb before washing, and pat each area dry before moving on. To finish, turn patient on their side and wash from the neck down to the buttocks.

Privacy is a priority when giving bed baths: always cover areas not being washed. Use new washcloths when moving to a new area, and change water when it is soapy, dirty, or cold. After the bath is complete, ensure that the areas between the toes, under the breasts, and inside skin folds are dry before dressing the patient.

Skills Evaluation: Give Modified Bed Bath (Face and One Arm, Hand and Underarm)

1. Wash hands.

2. Remove patient's gown and dispose of it properly. (Keep the patient's chest and lower body covered with a blanket.)

3. Test water temperature for safety and comfort.

4. Put on gloves.

5. Wash face with a wet facecloth with no soap. Begin with inner aspect of eyes and expand to the rest of the face. Use a new spot on the facecloth each time.

6. Dry face.

7. Uncover arm to be washed and place towel underneath.

8. Apply soap to washcloth and gently wash fingers, hand, arm, and underarm. Dry washed area.

9. Dress patient in a clean gown.

10. Clean, store, or dispose of linen and supplies appropriately, observing clean technique.

Patients who are able to leave their bed may take **tub baths**. The nurse aide may provide various levels of assistance. They may simply be present and available for help when asked, or they may need to assist the patient with bathing. Some guidelines for tub baths are given below:

- Always clean the tub before bathing a patient.
- Ensure side rails, call light, and other safety equipment are in working order before bringing patient to the tub.
- Ask the patient to void before starting the bath.
- Remove hearing aids and glasses before helping patient into bathtub.
- Monitor patient for weakness or dizziness.
- Tub baths should be no longer than 20 minutes.
- Check water temperature for safety and comfort.
- Never fill the tub higher than waist deep.
- Keep soap bar out of the water when not washing. Do not use oils in a tub or a shower.
- Use a nonskid mat for patient to stand on when they exit the tub.
- Use the same order as the bed bath, starting with the eyes and ending with the perineal area. Wet and shampoo hair if requested.

The main responsibility of the nurse aide when assisting with **showers** is to maintain the patient's safety. There is a greater risk of dizziness or falls if a patient stands to bathe.

Cleaning

Patients should use a bench or chair if they are a fall risk. There is also a risk for chills if the patient is not under the stream of water, especially with a handheld shower nozzle.

Guidelines for showers are similar to those for tub baths. Provide the requested amount of bathing assistance, and monitor for safety risks.

Perineal care should be done when bathing and whenever the patient has urine or feces on them. It prevents infection, promotes comfort, and prevents odors. Some general guidelines for perineal care are given below.

- For females, separate the labia with one hand, and wipe one side, the other side, then the middle with the other hand.
- For males, retract the foreskin if the patient is uncircumcised. Start at the meatus and wipe downward in a circular motion. Replace the foreskin when done.
- Always use a new area of the washcloth and a single stroke from top to bottom.
- Change washcloths when soiled. Do not reuse dirty washcloths or place them in the water basin.

Skills Evaluation: Provide Perineal Care (Peri-Care) for Female

1. Test water temperature in basin for safety and comfort.

2. Put on gloves.

3. Place pad under buttocks and perineal area.

4. Expose the patient's body from hips to knees.

5. Using soapy washcloth, wash perineal area, wiping front to back, using new area of washcloth each time.

6. With new wet washcloth, rinse the perineal area using the same method.

7. Dry perineal area with towel using the front-to-back method.

8. Roll patient to their side in the lateral or Sims'' position, and repeat procedure for rectal area.

9. Reposition patient in semi-Fowler's position and ensure comfort.

10. Clean, store, or dispose of linens and supplies appropriately, observing clean technique.

Bedmaking

Bedmaking promotes comfort and prevents skin breakdown and infections. Bed linen should be changed immediately when wet or dirty. If not visibly wet or soiled, linens should be changed once a day in acute

care and once a week in long-term care or in a patient's home. Bedmaking is usually done when the patient takes a bath or shower.

Beds are made differently based on the needs of the client.

- A **closed bed** is made for patients who are out of bed during the day.
- An **open bed** is ready for the patient to use.
- A **surgical bed** is prepared for patients being transferred from a stretcher.

When making any bed, the first step is to collect the linens in the order that they will be put on the bed. Carry linens away from body, and put clean linens down on clean and dry surfaces. Collected linens may include:

- bottom sheet
- top sheet
- blanket
- pillowcase for each pillow
- mattress pad, drawsheet, waterproof under-pad, or bed protector (as needed)

To make an **unoccupied bed**, start by removing dirty linens from the bed. Bag linens if they are contaminated and dispose of them properly. Used linens should never come in contact with the floor or furniture.

Make the bed starting with the bottom sheet (or mattress pad if requested). If using a flat sheet as a bottom sheet, use **mitered corners**. If a drawsheet or waterproof pad is being used, place it in position in the center of the bed. Place the top sheet and blanket on the bed, then tuck the top linens under the bottom of the bed using a mitered corner. Do not tuck in the sides of the top sheet or blanket.

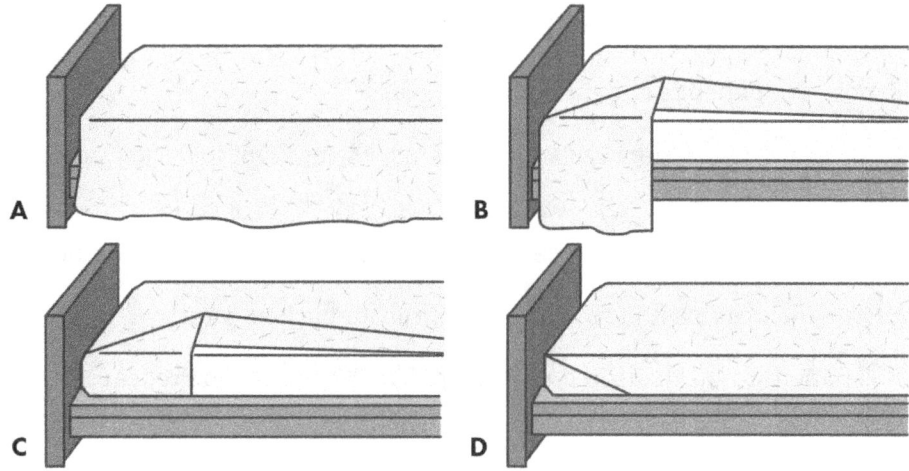

Then, put the pillow in the pillowcase and place on bed. When making a closed bed, the top linens are left unfolded (either over or under the pillow). When making an open bed, the top linens should be fan folded to the end of the bed.

> **HELPFUL HINT**
> Never shake linens or put linens on the floor.

To make an **occupied bed**, start by covering the patient with a bath blanket and removing the top sheet. Next, roll patient on their side and fan fold used linens toward the client. Place a clean bottom sheet and drawsheet (as needed) on the empty half of the bed and fan fold it toward the client.

The client can then be turned on their other side. Remove the dirty linens, and finish putting the bottom sheet and drawsheet on the bed. Shift patient to the supine position, and put on the top sheet and blanket. Tuck top linens under the bottom of the bed using a **toe pleat**.

> **HELPFUL HINT**
> When making an occupied bed, change gloves after touching dirty linens and before touching clean linens.

To make a surgical bed, put on the bottom sheet and top sheet. Next, fan fold the top sheet vertically to one side of the bed. Put the pillow in the pillowcase and place it to the side of the bed on a clean surface.

Quick Review Question

2. To remove the top sheet from an occupied bed, the nurse aide SHOULD:
    A) drape the patient with a bath blanket and remove the top sheet from underneath.
    B) roll the patient to their side facing away and fold the sheet toward the far rail.
    C) position the patient supine and fold the sheet toward the foot of the bed.
    D) assist the patient to a sitting position next to the bed and remove the top sheet.

Dressing and Grooming

Dressing

Undressing and dressing patients should be done with concern for the dignity and independence of the patient. Invite patients to participate to the extent of their abilities, and allow them to choose their own clothes when appropriate. Other guidelines for undressing and dressing patients are given below.

- Wash hands before starting.
- Remove garments on the stronger side first.
- Put clothes on the weaker side first.
- Support limbs as they are lifted or moved.
- When undressing and dressing a client in a bed, place them in the supine position.
- Cover undressed patients with a bath blanket.
- Dispose of soiled clothing appropriately.

Skills Evaluation: Apply One Knee-High Elastic Stocking

1. Position patient in the supine position.

2. Turn stocking inside out to the heel.

3. Place over patient's toes, and pull over patient's foot and leg.

4. Ensure heel of stocking is over heel, toe opening is over toes, and there are no twists or wrinkles.

5. Wash hands.

Skills Evaluation: Dress Client with Affected (Weak) Right Arm

1. Ask patient what shirt they would like to wear.

2. Carefully remove gown from the left arm and then from the right arm while avoiding exposure of patient's chest.

3. Dispose of gown in dirty linen container.

4. Carefully pull shirt over patient's head, and pull on the right sleeve and then the left sleeve.

5. Straighten shirt and reposition patient.

6. Wash hands.

Quick Review Question

3. Garments should be removed starting with the:
   A) weaker side.
   B) stronger side.
   C) right side.
   D) left side.

Hair Care

Brushing hair increases blood flow to the scalp and keeps hair from becoming matted. Provide hair care when it is needed or requested. Some general guidelines for brushing hair are given below.

- Wear gloves if there are scalp sores or a large amount of matting or dirt. z Be sure there are no broken or sharp bristles or teeth in the brush/comb. z Place a towel behind the patient's head or on their shoulders to catch falling hair.
- Comb curly or coarse hair starting from the nape and move upward, fluffing hair.
- Comb straight hair from the top of the head. Smooth hair downward.
- For hair tangles, hold hair with one hand above the tangle and comb out the tangle. Avoid pulling at the patient's scalp.

> **HELPFUL HINT**
>
> Always report any sores, hair loss, or the presence of nits or lice.

Shampooing hair may be done daily or a few times a month. Many long-term care residents have their hair washed on their bath day or in the hair salon. The tub or shower typically has a handheld spray that facilitates shampooing. For bedbound patients, some facilities have an inflatable basin to wash their hair in bed.

When shampooing, focus on patient safety by keeping water and soap out of the patient's eyes. (A washcloth may be used to cover their eyes.) Also make sure not to scrape or damage the scalp when massaging the shampoo into the hair. Remove items that may be damaged by water (e.g., hearing aids) before starting.

Safety is also an important focus when **shaving** patients. Safety razors may be used for most patients. However, patients at high risk for bleeding or skin injury (e.g., those with diabetes or bleeding disorders) may require the use of an electric razor. If bleeding occurs, apply pressure and report per facility policies.

> **HELPFUL HINT**
>
> Never leave water or lotion between a patient's toes.

Always moisten the area to be shaved before starting, and use shaving cream. Hold skin taut, and shave in the direction of hair growth except when shaving the legs or using a rotary shaver.

Quick Review Question

4. A nurse aide is brushing a client's hair and notices sores on the scalp. The nurse aide SHOULD:
   A) offer to shampoo the client's hair.
   B) tell the client to report the sores to their doctor.
   C) clean and bandage the sores.
   D) report the sores to the nurse.

Nail and Foot Care

Trimming nails prevents infections, odors, torn nails, and lacerations. For patients with conditions that impede healing (e.g., diabetes), a small injury in their foot can lead to serious complications. For this reason, most facilities do not allow nurse aides to trim nails. If the nurse aide is asked to trim nails, they should use caution if the patient has diabetes, circulation problems, an ingrown nail, or are on medications that cause bleeding. General guidelines for nail trimming are given below.

- Soak nails before trimming (5 to 10 minutes for fingernails; 15 to 20 minutes for toenails).
- Clean under nails with an orange stick. Clean the orange stick with a towel after each nail.
- Gently push back patient's cuticles with the orange stick.
- Clip nails straight across and file any roughness with an emery board.
- Apply lotion after hands or feet are clean and dry.
- Report to the nurse any injuries or signs of infection such as blisters or ingrown toenails.

Skills Evaluation: Provide Foot Care on One Foot

1. Check water temperature for safety and comfort.

2. Lay down protective barrier, and place basin where patient can put their foot in it.

3. Put on gloves.

4. Place patient's foot in the water.

5. Lift foot and wash with soapy washcloth.

6. Rinse foot with water.

7. Dry foot, ensuring areas between toes are dry.

8. Apply lotion to the foot (all areas except between toes).

9. Clean, store, or dispose of supplies using clean technique.

Quick Review Question

5. A nurse aide is trimming a patient's fingernails and cuts too deep, causing the client to bleed. The nurse aide SHOULD:
   A) clean and bandage the wound.
   B) leave the wound alone and get the nurse.
   C) apply pressure to the wound and alert the nurse.
   D) place the client's hand back in the water basin until the bleeding stops.

Nutrition and Hydration

Nutrition Basics

Food provides **nutrients**: the molecules that provide energy and the chemical building blocks the body needs to function. There are five main groups of nutrients.

- Carbohydrates are sugars that provide easily accessible energy for cells.
- Fats are molecules that store energy for later use.
- Proteins perform a wide range of functions in the body, including providing structural support in cells and tissues.
- Vitamins are molecules the body needs in small amounts to function but cannot make on its own.
- Minerals are elements (e.g., calcium) that the body requires to function.

People must eat a balance of different foods to meet their nutritional needs. The United

States Department of Agriculture (USDA) has created dietary guidelines called **MyPlate** to help people eat appropriate amounts of fruits, vegetables, grains, protein, and dairy foods.

Grains are foods made from wheat, rice, and other cereal crops. They are high in carbohydrates.

Fruits are the seed-bearing parts of plants. They provide essential vitamins and minerals and are low fat. However, they may contain high amounts of sugar.

Vegetables are the leaves, stalks, and roots of plants. They provide essential vitamins and minerals and are usually low in fat and sugar.

Dairy products are made from milk. They contain calcium and vitamin D, which are essential for bone health.

Protein can come from animal sources (e.g., beef) or plant sources (e.g., tofu).

Special diets are defined by their texture or the type of food they contain. Clients may require special diets to manage allergies, physical limitations, metabolic disorders, or medication interaction. They may also follow special diets for cultural or religious reasons.

> **HELPFUL HINT**
> Calories are a measure of the energy in food. Fats are the most calorie-dense nutrient (9 calories per gram).

- diabetic diet: strictly regulated carbohydrate consumption
- low-sodium diet: low in salt
- cardiac diet: restricted fat and salt
- clear liquid diet: liquids only, including water, clear broth, and popsicles
- full liquid diet: foods that become a liquid at body temperature such as ice cream or cooked cereal
- mechanical soft diet: semi-solid, easily digestible food like scrambled eggs and shredded meats
- residue-free diet: low in indigestible food like fiber and seeds
- high-fiber diet: high in fiber such as fruits and whole grains
- bland diet: low-fiber foods without strong spices such as white toast or cottage cheese
- high-calorie diet: intake of 3,000 or 4,000 calories a day
- limited-calorie diet: restricted calories to promote weight loss
- vegetarian diet: no meat
- vegan diet: no meat, dairy, or other animal products
- kosher diet: food prepared according to Jewish dietary laws
- halal diet: food prepared according to Islamic dietary laws

> **HELPFUL HINT**
> Dysphagia is difficulty swallowing. Clients with dysphagia may require a special diet (e.g., mechanically soft) to reduce the risk of choking.

> **HELPFUL HINT**
> Patients who have dysphagia will drink thickened liquids to prevent choking. Some liquids come ready-made in the proper consistency, while others must be prepared by the nurse aide.

Activities of Daily Living

Serving Suggestions

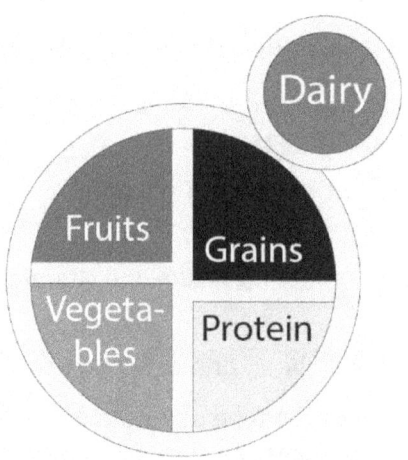

Quick Review Question

6. What type of diet might be ordered to help a patient with constipation?
   A) high fiber
   B) clear liquid
   C) vegetarian
   D) low sodium

Hydration Basics

Hydration is the balance of fluids in the body. Adequate fluid intake prevents conditions related to dehydration, including constipation, urinary tract infections, dizziness, and heart problems.

Fluid balance is often assessed by measuring a client's **intake and output (I&O)**. Input is all the fluids the client consumes; output is all the fluid excreted from the body. Intake and output are measured in milliliters (mL). Common conversion amounts for intake include:

- $1\ teaspoon\ =\ 5\ mL$
- $1\ tablespoon\ =\ 15\ mL$
- $1\ ounce\ =\ 30\ mL$
- $1\ cup\ =\ 240\ mL$
- $1\ pint\ =\ 500\ mL$

Some patients have special orders affecting their intake of fluids. **NPO** is an abbreviation of the Latin phrase *nil per os* and means "nothing by mouth." Patients on NPO cannot eat or drink. **Encourage fluids** means that something to drink should be offered as often as possible and be kept within reach. Patients listed as **restrict fluids** are allowed a limited amount of fluids determined by the doctor.

Activities of Daily Living

Quick Review Question

7. A patient who is NPO asks the nurse aide for a lunch tray. The nurse aide SHOULD:
   A) tell the patient they cannot eat any food and alert the nurse to the patient's request.
   B) offer the patient a glass of water instead.
   C) leave a lunch tray but tell the patient to talk to their nurse before eating.
   D) offer a snack but tell the patient they cannot tell the nurse they ate.

Assisting With Meals

When assisting patients with meals, the nurse aide should focus on patient safety and independence. Many patients who require assistance to eat may have difficulties with chewing or swallowing, so the nurse aide should continually monitor for choking. The nurse aide should also follow protocols to ensure patients on special diets eat the appropriate food.

Patients require varying levels of assistance with eating. The nurse aide should encourage independence by having the patient participate as much as possible. Patients may be able to select which foods they want, eat some foods by hand, or hold certain utensils or cups.

Other general guidelines for feeding are given below.

- Match patient's name to name on food tray and check allergies.
- Sit facing the patient to watch for signs of choking.
- Report signs of difficulty swallowing to the nurse.
- Review the contents of the tray with the patient, and ask what they would prefer to eat first. Defer to the patient's preferences.
- Use a spoon to prevent injuries. Bites of food should be $\frac{1}{2}$ of the spoon or smaller.
- Ensure mouth is empty before offering another bite of food. Do not rush the patient.
- For patients with impaired vision, describe what is on their plate and where it is using a clock pattern.
- Encourage patient to drink fluids by offering fluids throughout the meal.
- Never give a patient a cup with hot liquid in it.
- Wipe patient's face with a napkin when needed.
- At the end of the meal, verify patient is full and document the percentage eaten.

Skills Evaluation: Feed Client Who Cannot Feed Self

1. Match patient's name with name on tray.
2. Place patient in upright position (high Fowler's).
3. Place tray where patient can see it easily.
4. Clean patient's hands.
5. Sit facing the patient.

Skills Evaluation: Feed Client Who Cannot Feed Self

6. Identify food on the tray, and ask what the patient wants to eat first.

7. Using a spoon, offer patient a bite of each food. Identify each food when offered.

8. Offer beverages at least once during the meal.

9. Ask patient if they are ready for another bite of food before giving it.

10. When done, clean patient's hands and mouth.

11. Wash hands.

Quick Review Question

8. When feeding a client, the nurse aide SHOULD offer fluids:
    A) only at the beginning of the meal.
    B) only at the end of the meal.
    C) regularly throughout the meal.
    D) after each bite of food.

Elimination

Assisting With Elimination

A **bedpan** is used for elimination when a patient cannot get out of bed. The bedpan is positioned under the patient when they need to urinate or have a bowel movement. Most patients will use a regular bedpan, but patients with hip or spinal injuries may use a **fracture pan**.

1. Place protective barrier and bedpan under patient's buttocks.

2. Remove gloves and wash hands.

3. Raise head of bed.

4. Place toilet tissue, call light, and hand wipes within reach.

5. Ask patient to use hand wipes and press call light when done.

6. When patient presses call light, wash hands and put on gloves.

7. Lower head of bed.

8. Ask patient to lift buttocks or roll patient to their side and remove bedpan.

9. Empty bedpan into toilet. Rinse bedpan and pour rinse into toilet.

10. Place bedpan in appropriate dirty supply area.

11. Remove gloves and wash hands.

> ### Skills Evaluation: Assist with Use of Bedpan
>
> 1. Lower head of bed.
> 2. Put on gloves.
> 3. Cover patient with a blanket.

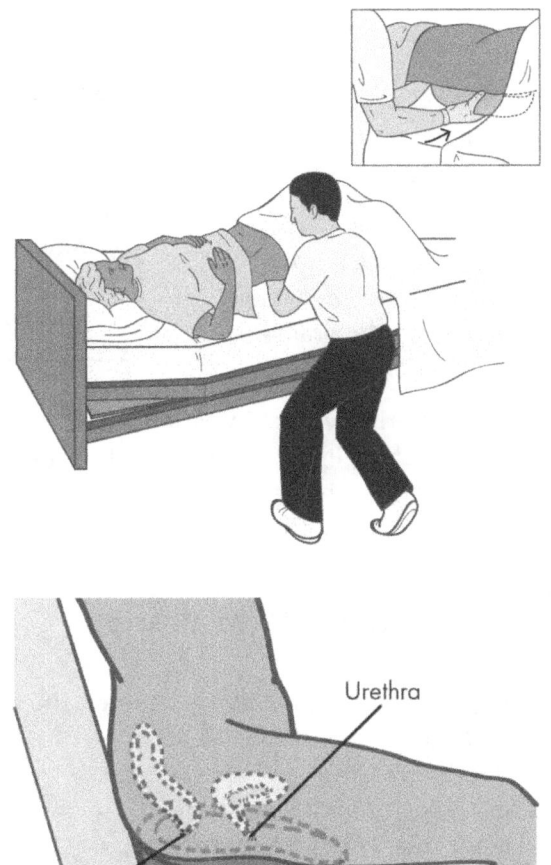

Men use **urinals** to void urine in bed. The nurse aide may need to assist the patient by bringing the urinal to the patient, assisting them into a sitting position, or positioning the urinal for the patient. When the patient is done, the nurse aide should note the output and empty the urinal into the toilet. Follow appropriate protocol to ensure urine does not contaminate clean surfaces.

If the patient can stand and transfer, they may use a **commode**. The commode should be positioned next to and facing the foot of the bed like a wheelchair. The nurse aide should make sure the wheels on the commode are locked before the patient leaves the bed. The patient can be assisted into and off the commode similar to a chair.

Activities of Daily Living

Incontinence products include adult diapers, liners, and protective pads (disposable or reusable) with an absorbent layer on one side and a moisture barrier on the other. Incontinence is a major cause of skin irritation, and most patients require a moisture barrier cream when using incontinence products.

Quick Review Question

9. Moisture barrier cream should be applied to a patient's perineal area:
    A) before a clean incontinence product is applied.
    B) before they use a commode.
    C) after they use bedpan for a bowel movement.
    D) after a condom catheter has been secured.

Urinary Catheters

Indwelling catheters (or Foley catheters) are inserted through the urethra into the bladder to continuously drain urine. The urine is collected in a **drainage bag**, which may be attached to the patient's leg or bed.

Drainage bags must be emptied regularly. The amount of urine in the drainage bag may need to be recorded as part of I&O. This may be done through a gauge on the drainage bag or by draining urine from the bag into a graduate.

> **HELPFUL HINT**
> Urinary collection bags are used to collect urine samples from pediatric patients. The adhesive bag is sealed around the baby's genitals and removed once enough urine has been collected.

Indwelling catheters create a high risk of **urinary tract infection (UTI)**, so the nurse aide must be meticulous when cleaning catheters and changing drainage bags. The connection between the catheter and drainage tube should be sterile. When reconnecting the drainage bag, the ends must be wiped with antiseptic. When changing a bag, do not touch the sterile cap or plug that connects the catheter to the drainage bag.

Quick Review Question

10. When reconnecting the drainage tube to an indwelling catheter, the nurse aide SHOULD:
    A) clean the inside of the drainage tube with soapy water.
    B) secure the drainage tube to the catheter with elastic tape.
    C) hang the drainage bag above the level of the bladder.
    D) wipe the end of the drainage tube with an antiseptic wipe.

Catheter care includes cleaning the exposed portion of the catheter from the meatus. Clean at least 4 inches of the tube. Catheter care may also include perineal cleaning.

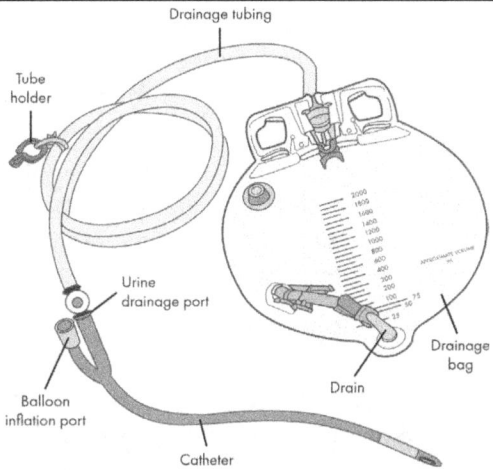

Skills Evaluation: Provide Catheter Care for Female

1. Check temperature of water for safety and comfort.

2. Put on gloves.

3. Place protective barrier under buttocks.

4. Expose patient between hips and knees.

5. Stabilize the catheter with one hand being careful not to pull it.

6. Use a soapy washcloth and wipe downward, away from the meatus, at least 4 inches. Use a clean section of the washcloth for each wipe.

7. Use the same procedure to rinse and then dry the catheter.

8. Cover and reposition the patient.

9. Clean, store, and dispose of supplies appropriately.

Condom catheters are secured over the penis with elastic tape to catch urine. They should be changed daily as part of perineal care. Use only the tape provided by the manufacturer to secure the catheter—other types of adhesives may restrict blood flow to the penis. To apply a condom catheter, hold the penis firmly while unrolling the condom and leave a space of one inch at the tip of the condom.

Bowel Elimination

Fecal impaction occurs when a patient has had long-term constipation. Notify the nurse if the patient has no stools, loose stools, abdominal pain, or distension. The nurse may do a digital rectal exam to check for an impaction. The doctor may order laxatives, suppositories, or an enema to encourage bowel elimination. The nurse may remove the impaction, or they may ask the nurse aide to remove it.

To remove the impaction, place the patient in Sims" position. Insert a lubricated, gloved finger into the rectum, massage around the hardened feces, and gently pull a small amount out.

Removing impacted feces in the rectum can be dangerous. It may stimulate the vagus nerve, cause a perforation, or cause bleeding. Stop the procedure and report to the nurse if the patient bleeds, has an irregular pulse, loses consciousness, or experiences pain.

Activities of Daily Living

Enemas are liquids that stimulate movement of the bowels. The type of fluid used is determined by the physician. (Nurses must administer enemas containing medications.) Enemas are administered with the patient in Sims' position. The lubricated tip of the enema tube is inserted into the rectum, and the fluid is slowly drained into the rectum. After an enema, the nurse aide should be prepared to provide the patient with a bedpan or commode, or to move them to the toilet so they can defecate.

> **HELPFUL HINT**
> **Suppositories** are medications absorbed in the rectum. Because they are medications, suppositories are inserted by nurses. However, the nurse aide may be asked to assist.

Ostomies are openings that allow drainage from organs (e.g., bladder, intestine) outside the body. The opening on the skin's surface is called a **stoma**. Ostomies typically empty into an **ostomy bag** that can be opened at the bottom to be drained into the toilet. The ostomy bag is changed every 2 to 7 days.

Quick Review Question

11. After a patient receives an enema, the nurse aide should be prepared to:
    A) keep the patient NPO for 8 hours.
    B) place the patient in high Fowler's position.
    C) provide the patient with a meal tray.
    D) assist the patient with bowel elimination.

Patient Comfort and Safety

The nurse aide has a duty to help patients feel safe and comfortable. When performing tasks with patients, the nurse aide should always prioritize these needs. Patients may also tell the nurse aide when they are uncomfortable or have unmet needs. The nurse aide should meet these requests when able and should report complaints of pain or inadequate care to the nurse.

Some other guidelines for promoting patient safety and comfort are below.

- Defer to the patient regarding any personal preferences or rituals.
- Position the patient properly.
- Keep the patient's clothes and bed linens clean and wrinkle-free.
- Adjust the room temperature and lighting levels per the patient's request.
- Organize patient care tasks so the patient's sleep is uninterrupted.
- Provide a calm, dark environment for sleep.
- Use a gentle touch and a soft voice when providing care.
- Avoid sudden movements and loud noises.
- Facilitate patient visits with supportive family.

Quick Review Question

12. A client who is having his vital signs checked every four hours complains to the nurse aide that he cannot get enough sleep. How should the nurse aide respond?
    A) "Everyone has to have their vital signs taken at night."
    B) "I'm sorry you are not getting enough sleep. I will speak with the nurse about changing your schedule."
    C) "Sleep is very important. I will stop taking your vital signs at night and instead come in the morning."
    D) "I'm sorry, but I can't change your schedule. Maybe you can take a nap during the day."

Fall Prevention

Falls are the most common cause of injury in medical care. Fall risk is increased by many different factors, including increased age and certain medical conditions. Follow general fall risk guidelines for all patients, regardless of risk.

- Keep floor clear of clutter.
- Ensure patient's basic needs are met (e.g., they are hydrated, they can eliminate as needed).
- Place call light and equipment (e.g., eyeglasses, canes) within the patient's reach.
- Respond to call lights and alarms promptly.
- Use side rails and wheel locks on beds and stretchers.
- Keep the patient's bed in the appropriate position.
- Use the necessary staff and equipment for providing care.
- Ensure patients wear non-slip footwear.
- Do a safety check of the patient's room after visitors leave.

> **HELPFUL HINT**
> Never use one patient's equipment with another patient.

Quick Review Question

13. All of the following are responsibilities of the nurse aide related to fall prevention EXCEPT:
    A) picking up clutter from the room floor.
    B) putting up side rails after transferring a patient to the bed.
    C) monitoring the patient's sedation level.
    D) providing nonslip footwear for the patient.

Lifting, Transferring, and Positioning Patients

The nurse aide needs to know how to safely move and position patients in the bed and how to **transfer** patients to and from the bed. Always follow general safety guidelines for lifting and transferring patients, regardless of the patient's functional status.

- Know the procedure, equipment, and number of staff needed for the move/ transfer before starting.
- Promote patient participation when appropriate. It provides the patient with a sense of autonomy and minimizes the strain on the caregiver's body.
- Always bend at knees (not at waist) when lifting.
- Stop the move/transfer and return patient to original position if they report pain.
- Use a predetermined signal (e.g., on the count of three) to start the lift.
- Keep the patient's body in a comfortable and correctly aligned position when moving/transferring.
- Always lock the wheels on beds, stretchers, and wheelchairs when moving/ transferring patients.
- Use appropriate position devices to promote comfort and prevent injury (e.g., pressure ulcers).

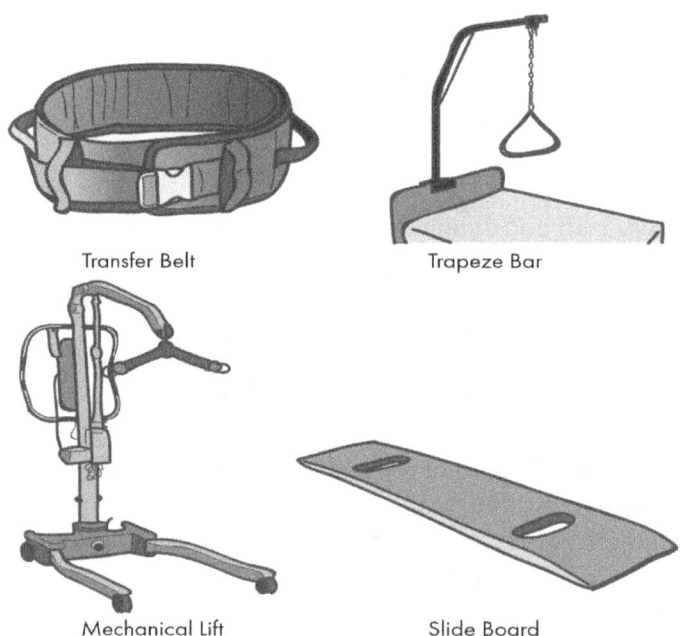

Transfer Belt

Trapeze Bar

Mechanical Lift

Slide Board

Activities of Daily Living

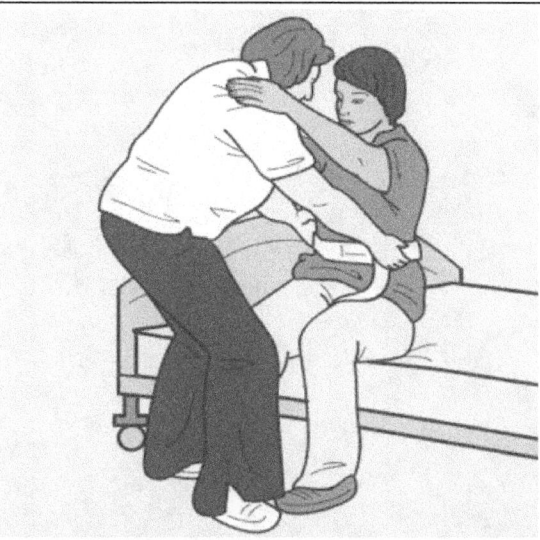

Skills Evaluation: Assist to Ambulate Using Transfer Belt

1. Ensure client is wearing non-skid footwear.

2. Lower bed to a safe level and lock wheels.

3. Assist patient into a sitting position with feet flat on the floor.

4. Apply transfer belt securely over clothing.

5. Explain procedure to patient and agree on a signal to begin standing.

6. Stand facing patient (knee to knee or toe to toe) with an upward grasp on the transfer belt at the patient's sides.

7. Direct patient to stand using an agreed-upon signal.

8. Assist patient to stand.

9. Walk behind and slightly to the side of the patient for at least 10 feet.

10. Assist patient back into bed and remove the belt.

11. Wash hands.

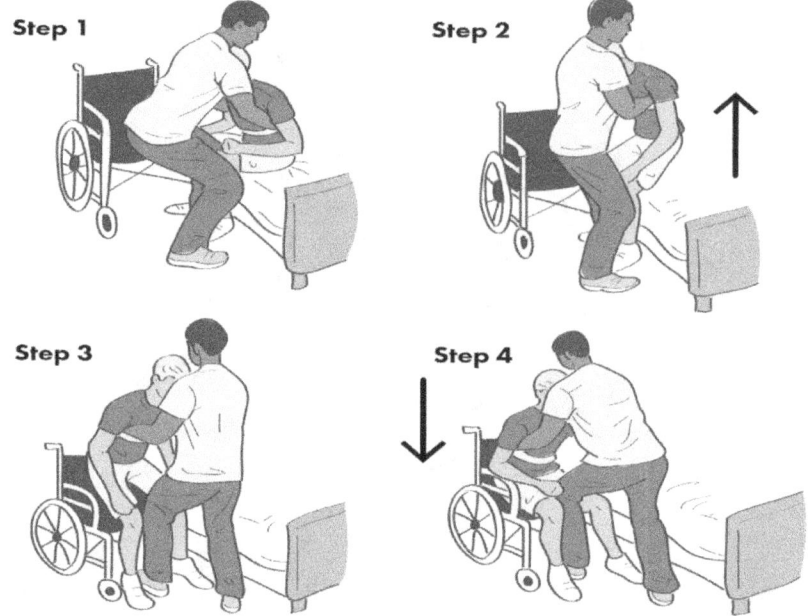

Skills Evaluation: Transfer from Bed to Wheelchair Using Transfer Belt

1. Position wheelchair alongside the bed facing the head or the foot of the bed.

2. Fold up or remove the footrests on the wheelchair.

3. Lock wheelchair wheels.

4. Lower the bed to a safe level and lock bed wheels.

5. Assist patient into a sitting position with feet flat on the floor.

6. Ensure patient is wearing non-slip shoes.

7. Fasten transfer belt at patient's waist over their clothes.

8. Explain the procedure to the patient and agree on a signal to begin standing.

9. Stand facing patient (knee to knee or toe to toe) with an upward grasp on the transfer belt at the patient's sides.

10. Direct patient to stand using an agreed-upon signal.

11. Help client position themselves in front of the wheelchair with the back of their legs against the wheelchair.

12. Help patient sit down with hips against the back of the wheelchair.

13. Remove transfer belt.

14. Reapply footrests and position patient.

15. Wash hands.

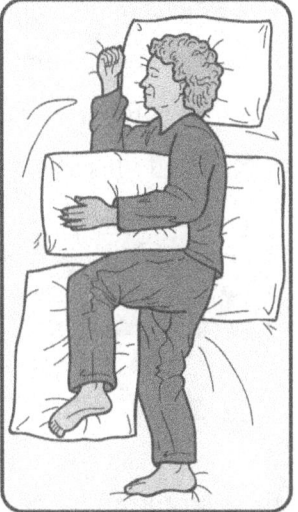

> **HELPFUL HINT**
>
> *Abduction* is movement of a limb away from the body. *Adduction* is the movement of a limb toward the body.

Skills Evaluation: Position on Side

1. Lower the head of the bed.

2. Raise rail on the side of the bed the patient will turn toward.

3. Ask patient to reach for the side rail if able, while assisting them to slowly roll onto their side.

4. Place pillow under patient's head.

5. Reposition patient's shoulder and arm so patient is not laying on arm.

6. Place pillow behind client's back.

7. Bend patient's knee and place pillow between their legs and under knee and ankle for support.

8. Wash hands.

Quick Review Question

14. If a patient complains of pain while being transferred from a bed to a wheelchair, the nurse aide SHOULD:
    A) tell the patient they will document the pain in the patient's chart.
    B) ignore the patient's complaint and continue the transfer.
    C) immediately stop the transfer and return the patient to bed.
    D) try to complete the transfer using a different procedure.

Range of Motion Exercises

Range of motion (ROM) exercises are the movement of extremities through the full range of their natural motion (without causing pain). ROM exercises strengthen muscles and prevent muscle degradation caused by lack of movement. **Active ROM exercises** can be done by the patient alone. During **passive ROM exercises**, the nurse aide moves the limb through the ROM with little or no help from the patient. General guidelines for ROM exercises are given below.

- Move patient's limbs slowly and gently at joints to prevent injury.
- Only move as far as the patient is able to do so comfortably.
- Support limbs at joints (elbows and wrist for arms, knees and ankles for legs).
- ROM exercises should never be forced. If the patient experiences pain or discomfort, stop exercise immediately.

Skills Evaluation: Perform Modified Passive Range of Motion (PROM) for One Knee and One Ankle

1. Place patient in the supine position.

2. Ask patient to voice complaints of pain.

3. Support leg at knee and ankle and gently bend and straighten patient's leg at the knee three times. (Stop exercise if patient complains of pain.)

4. Lift patient's foot a few inches off the bed, supporting their ankle, and push/pull foot three times. (Stop exercise if patient complains of pain.)

5. Wash hands.

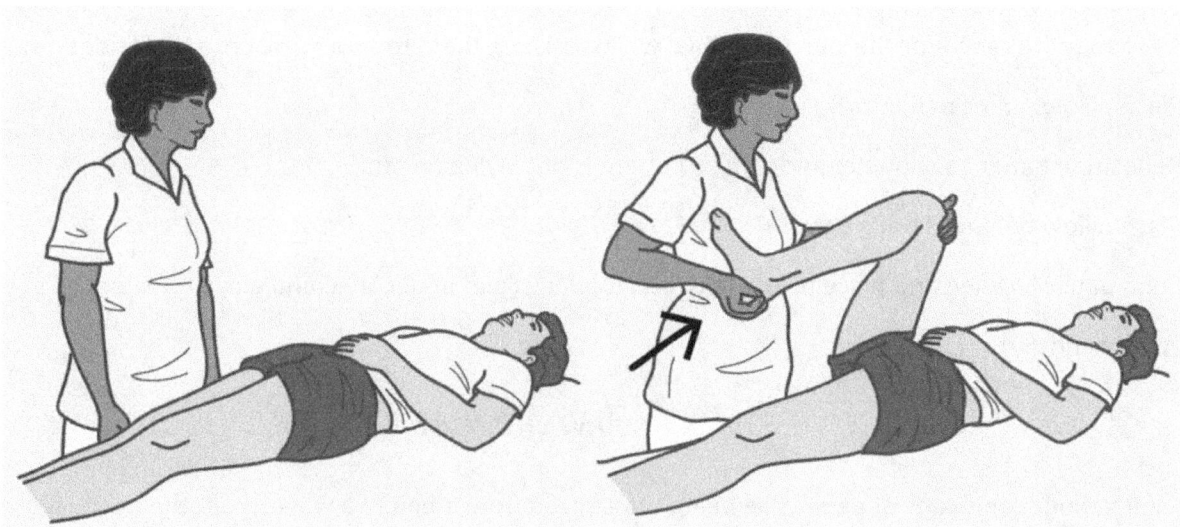

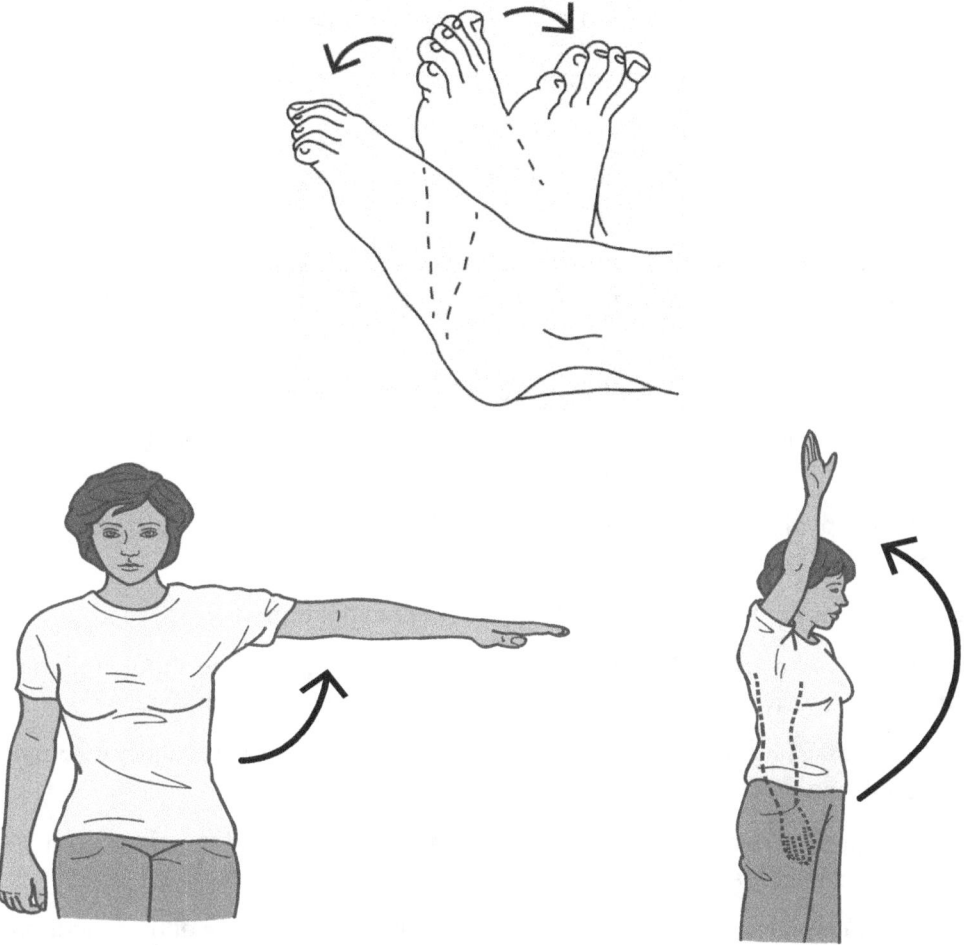

Skills Evaluation: Perform Modified Passive Range of Motion (PROM) for One Shoulder

1. Instruct patient to voice complaints of pain.

2. Support arm at elbow and wrist, and gently lift straight arm up toward the patient's head until it is level with their ear. Repeat three times. (Stop exercise if patient complains of pain.)

3. Support arm at elbow and wrist, and gently lift straight arm away from the patient's body until it reaches shoulder level. Repeat three times. (Stop exercise if patient complains of pain.)

4. Wash hands.

Quick Review Question

15. When performing passive ROM exercises for the knee, the patient should be:
    A) supine.
    B) prone.
    C) sitting on the edge of the bed.
    D) standing next to a chair.

Activities of Daily Living

ANSWER KEY

1. B) is correct. Clean dentures should be put in a cup of water or solution and placed within reach of the patient.

2. A) is correct. To remove the top sheet from an occupied bed, the nurse aide should drape the patient with a bath blanket and remove the top sheet from underneath. This allows the patient to remain covered.

3. B) is correct. Clothing should be removed starting with the stronger side.

4. D) is correct. When the nurse aide notices any change in skin condition, including sores on the scalp, they should notify the nurse.

5. C) is correct. The nurse aide should apply pressure to the wound to prevent further bleeding and immediately notify the nurse.

6. A) is correct. Diets that are high in fiber can help relieve constipation.

7. A) is correct. Patients who are NPO should not eat or drink. The nurse aide should tell the patient they cannot give them a lunch tray and alert the nurse so she can talk with the patient.

8. C) is correct. When assisting clients with eating, fluids should be offered regularly throughout the meal to help patients chew and swallow foods.

9. A) is correct. Moisture barrier cream is used with incontinence products to help prevent skin damage caused by moisture and bacteria.

10. D) is correct. To reconnect a drainage tube to an indwelling catheter, the end of the drainage tube should be wiped with antiseptic to prevent infection.

11. D) is correct. After receiving an enema, patients will need to defecate. The nurse aide should be prepared to assist the patient with a bedpan or commode, or to move them to the toilet.

12. B) is correct. The nurse aide should show sympathy to the patient. The nurse aide cannot change the patient's schedule on their own, but they can offer to speak to the nurse about it.

13. C) is correct. The patient's sedation level will be monitored by a nurse.

14. C) is correct. Moves and transfers should be stopped for any new complaints of pain. In addition, the nurse should be notified so modifications can be made to the care plan.

15. A) is correct. Passive ROM exercises for the knee are done with the patient supine in the bed.

Basic Nursing Skills

The Physical Exam

The purpose of the patient **physical examination** is to assess the patient's health. The nurse aide's role in the physical exam may include preparing the room, greeting the patient, and taking vital signs. Specific tasks may include:

- collecting necessary equipment
- positioning and draping/gowning the patient
- disposing of used equipment
- escorting the patient to the exam room
- assisting with the exam (e.g., providing equipment)
- cleaning the exam room

During this process, the nurse aide should provide the patient with a sense of support and security. The nurse aide should explain each step to the patient and provide for their privacy (e.g., closing curtains).

Quick Review Question

1. When an alert and mobile patient needs to be draped for an exam, the nurse aide should:
    A) position the drape on the patient after they have undressed.
    B) instruct the patient on how to position the drape and leave the room while they undress.
    C) ask the nurse to place the drape on the patient.
    D) leave the door open to ensure the patient has placed the drape correctly.

Positioning Patients

The medical assistant should position the patient appropriately for different types of exams. These positions are discussed in Table 2.1.

Table 2.1. Medical Examination Positions

Position	Description	Image
Lateral	Patient is lying on side with right side on the bed (right lateral) or left side on the bed (left lateral). Pillows are placed behind the patient's back and under the knee, head, and neck. Lateral position is used for patient comfort and to prevent injuries from long-term bedrest.	

Table 2.1. Medical Examination Positions

Position	Description	Image
Supine	Patient lies on their back with arms to the sides. Supine positions are used during many surgical procedures, while performing an ECG, and for obtaining orthostatic blood pressure.	
Dorsal recumbent	Patient lies on their back with knees bent and feet flat on the table. Dorsal recumbent positions are used for gynecological exams.	
Lithotomy	Patient lies on their back with buttocks on the edge of the lower end of the table, legs elevated, and feet in stirrups. Lithotomy position is used for gynecological exams, childbirth, and some surgeries. position is	
Sims	Patient lies on their left side with the left leg flexed, left arm resting behind the body, right leg flexed, and right arm at the chest. Sims' position is used for taking the temperature rectally, rectal examinations, and administering enemas.	

Basic Nursing Skills

Table 2.1. Medical Examination Positions		
Position	Description	Image
Prone	Patient lies on their stomach. Prone position is used to examine the spine and for chiropractic procedures.	
Fowler's	Patient lies faceup with their upper body elevated at 45 to 60 degrees. Fowler's position is used in barium swallow procedures, nasopharyngeal feedings, and respiratory distress.	
Semi-Fowler's	Same as Fowler's position, except the upper body is only elevated between 30 and 45 degrees. Semi-Fowler's position is used for nasogastric feedings, X-rays, and respiratory distress.	

Quick Review Question

2. The nurse has asked the nurse aide to place a patient in Fowler's position. The nurse aide should position the head of the bed:
   A) flat.
   B) at a 30° angle.
   C) at a 45° angle.
   D) at a 90° angle.

Vital Signs

Body Temperature

HELPFUL HINT
Rectal temperature is taken with the patient in Sims' position.

Body temperature can be measured with a thermometer by various routes (see Table 2.2). Elevated temperature, or **fever**, is defined as a temperature higher than 100.4°F (38°C) (although this is not a universal standard—some physicians may use a different cutoff temperature). **Hypothermia** (body temperature below 95°F or 35°C) can occur when the body is exposed to cold weather or due to medical conditions such as a thyroid disorder.

Table 2.2. Measuring Body Temperature

Method	Location	Baseline
Axillary	armpit	97.6°F (36.5°C)
Oral	under tongue	98.6°F (37.0°C)
Rectal	rectum	99.6°F (37.5°C)
Temporal artery	forehead	99.6°F (37.5°C)
Tympanic membrane	inside ear	98.6°F (37.0°C)

Quick Review Question

3. To take a patient's temperature at the temporal artery, the nurse aide should place the thermometer:
   A) in the ear.
   B) in the rectum.
   C) on the forehead.
   D) under the tongue.

Pulse

The **pulse**, or **heart rate**, is the number of times the heart beats per minute. The average adult's pulse rate at rest is between 60 and 100 beats per minute. The pulse can be taken at a number of locations on the body.

- carotid pulse: to the side of the trachea
- radial pulse: on the thumb side of the inner wrist
- apical pulse: at the apex of the heart (with stethoscope)
- brachial pulse: on the side of the crease of the elbow
- pedal pulse: on the top of the foot

Basic Nursing Skills

Skills Evaluation: Counts and Records Radial Pulse

1. Explain procedure to patient.

2. Locate radial pulse with fingertips.

3. Count the beats for 1 minute.

4. Wash hands.

5. Record pulse.

Note: To pass this skill, you will need to record a pulse rate within 4 beats of the rate recorded by the evaluator.

> **HELPFUL HINT**
> Heart rate can also be found on the readouts of equipment used to test cardiovascular performance, including pulse oximeters and electrocardiograms (ECGs).

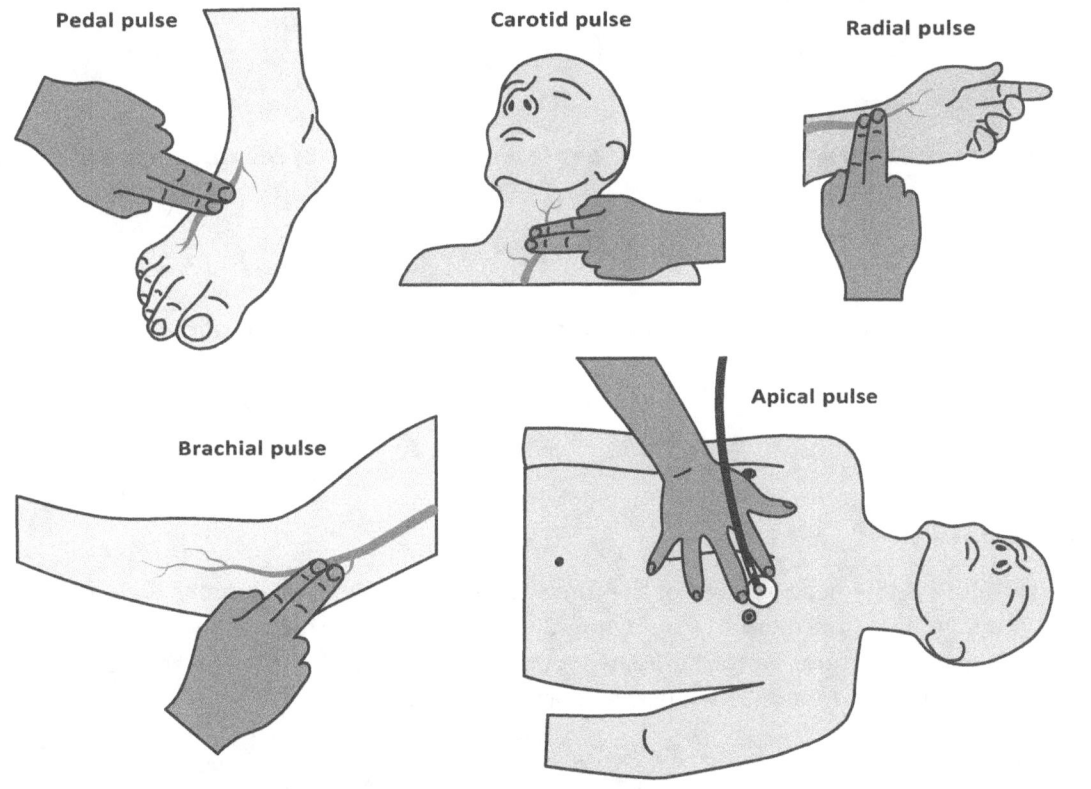

Basic Nursing Skills

> **Quick Review Question**
>
> 4. The carotid pulse can be palpated at which of the following locations on the body?
>   A) the anterior wrist
>   B) lateral to the trachea
>   C) in the groin
>   D) on the dorsum of the foot

Respiratory Rate

A person's **respiratory rate (RR)** is the number of breaths taken per minute. Respiratory rate is usually found by having the patient lie on their back (although this is not required) and counting the rise and fall of their chest. For an accurate measurement, the patient should be allowed to rest before the respiratory rate is measured. A normal adult's RR is 12 to 20 breaths per minute, although this rate can vary in children and adults over 65.

Skills Evaluation: Counts and Records Respirations

1. Explain procedure to patient.
2. Count patient's respirations for 1 minute.
3. Wash hands.
4. Record respirations.

Note: To pass this skill, you will need to record a rate within 2 breaths of the rate recorded by the evaluator.

> **Quick Review Question**
>
> 5. What position should a patient be in when the nurse aide measures respiratory rate?
>   A) Sims
>   B) lateral
>   C) prone
>   D) supine

Blood Pressure

Blood pressure (BP) is the measurement of the force of blood as it flows against the walls of the arteries. BP is measured in mm Hg (millimeters of mercury). Blood pressure is written as two numbers: systolic pressure and diastolic pressure. **Systolic pressure** is the pressure that occurs while the heart is contracting; **diastolic pressure** occurs while the heart is relaxed.

Skills Evaluation: Measures and Records Manual Blood Pressure

1. Explain procedure to patient.
2. Wipe stethoscope with alcohol.
3. Position patient with palm up and locate brachial artery.
4. Place cuff on client's upper arm with sensor over brachial artery.

Basic Nursing Skills

5. Position stethoscope over brachial artery.

6. Inflate cuff between 160 mm Hg and 180 mm Hg. (If sounds are heard immediately, deflate cuff and reinflate to 200 mm Hg.)

7. Note systolic pressure (first sound) and diastolic pressure (last sound).

8. Remove cuff.

9. Wash hands.

10. Record BP.

A healthy blood pressure has a systolic value of 100 to 139 mm Hg and a diastolic value of 60 to 79 mm Hg. High blood pressure is called **hypertension**; low blood pressure is **hypotension**.

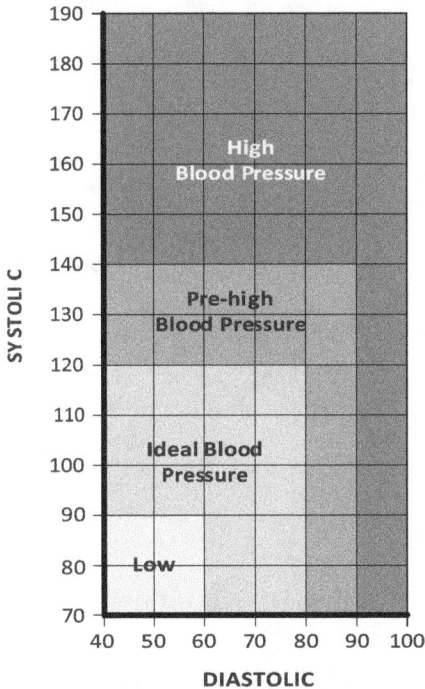

Blood pressure can be taken manually using a blood pressure cuff and stethoscope or by using an automatic or semiautomatic blood pressure monitor. (Both the cuff and electronic monitors are referred to as **sphygmomanometers**.) For both methods, the patient should be upright, with their feet on the floor and uncrossed, and the arm being used for the measurement should be at heart height.

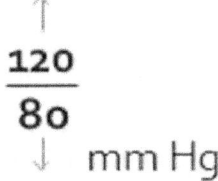

Basic Nursing Skills

> **HELPFUL HINT**
> *Korotkoff sounds* occur as the BP cuff is deflated. The first sound is the systolic pressure, and the last (fifth) sound is the diastolic pressure.

Note: To pass this skill, you will need to record a systolic and diastolic BP within 2 mm Hg of the BP found by the evaluator.

To use an automatic blood pressure monitor, the nurse aide wraps the cuff around the patient's upper arm and turns on the monitor. It will automatically inflate, deflate, and provide a pressure reading. A semiautomatic monitor requires manual inflation but will automatically deflate and provide a pressure reading.

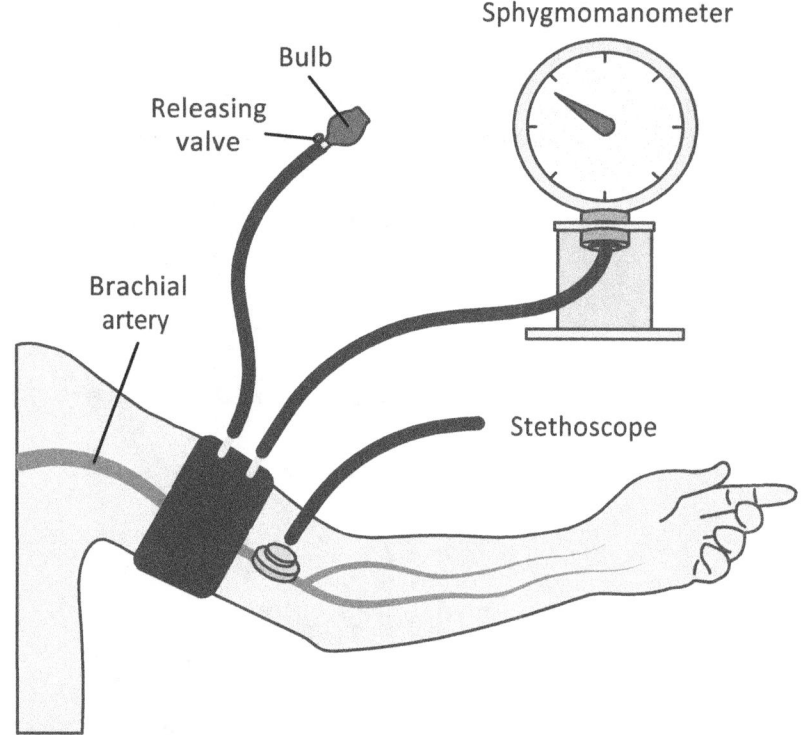

Quick Review Question

6. When using a sphygmomanometer to take a manual blood pressure, where is the stethoscope most commonly placed?
    A) carotid pulse
    B) dorsalis pedis pulse
    C) radial pulse
    D) brachial pulse

Height and Weight

The patient's **height** is assessed by using a fixed bar on the weight scale or wall. Height measurements are recorded in feet (ft) and inches (in) or in centimeters (cm).

The patient's **weight** is measured using a balanced scale and recorded in pounds (lb) or kilograms (kg). To convert between units for height and weight, multiply using the conversion factors given in Table 2.3.

Basic Nursing Skills

Table 2.3. Converting Units

Original unit	Operation	New unit
Pounds	divide by 2.2	kilograms
Kilograms	multiply by 2.2	pounds
Inches	multiply by 2.54	centimeters
Centimeters	divide by 2.54	inches

$12 \text{ inches} = 1 \text{ foot}$
$100 \text{ centimeters} = 1 \text{ meter}$
$16 \text{ ounces} = 1 \text{ pound}$

Skills Evaluation: Measures and Records Weight of Ambulatory Client

1. Explain procedure to patient.
2. Ensure patient is wearing nonskid footwear.
3. Set scale to zero.
4. Ask client to step on scale and read the weight.
5. Ask client to step off scale.
6. Wash hands.
7. Record weight.

Note: To pass this skill, you will need to record a weight within 2 pounds (0.9 kg) of the weight found by the evaluator.

Quick Review Question

7. According to the scale, an infant weighs 4.3 kg. What is the infant's weight in pounds?
   A) 1.95 lbs
   B) 5.2 lbs
   C) 8.6 lbs
   D) 9.46 lbs

Oxygen Saturation and Pulse Oximetry

Oxygen saturation is a measurement of the amount of oxygen in the blood. Specifically, it measures the amount of oxygen-saturated hemoglobin (the substance in red blood cells that carries oxygen) relative to unsaturated hemoglobin. Normal blood oxygen level is 94 to 100 percent. Oxygen saturation is measured

using a **pulse oximeter**, which is usually placed on the patient's finger. When the patient's finger is not accessible, the oximeter can be placed on the big toe or earlobe.

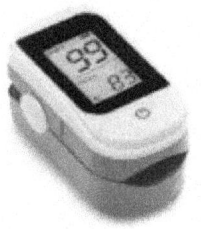

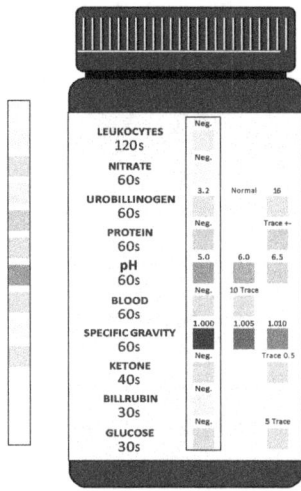

Quick Review Question

8. Pulse oximetry can be measured on a patient at all of the following locations EXCEPT:
   A) a finger.
   B) the abdomen.
   C) the big toe.
   D) an earlobe.

Specimen Collection and Testing

Urine and Stool

Urine can be used to test for a wide variety of conditions, including pregnancy, infections, metabolic disorders (e.g., diabetes), organ dysfunction, and cancers. Urine can be collected at random times or at a specific time. ⌘ **Random** urine samples are not taken at a scheduled time.

A **first morning** urine sample is collected before the patient takes in any fluid so that the urine is more concentrated (usually after 8 hours of sleep).

A **timed** urinalysis can span 2 to 72 hours. (A 24-hour specimen is the most common.)

Urine is collected over the given time period and added to a large collection container.

The patient should discard their first morning urine and start collecting urine after that.

Most urine samples are **voided** (passed from the body). A **regular voided sample** can be collected by the patient without any special preparations. **Double voiding** requires the patient to discard their first morning urine and wait a set amount of time (usually 30 minutes) to collect a sample. A **midstream clean catch** is collected after the perianal region has been cleaned with an antiseptic wipe and the patient has already voided a small amount of urine.

Skills Evaluation: Measures and Records Urinary Output

1. Put on gloves.
2. Pour urine from bedpan into measuring container.
3. Rinse bedpan and pour rinse water into toilet.
4. Measure urine in container.
5. Empty measuring container into toilet.
6. Rinse measuring container and pour rinse water into toilet.
7. Remove gloves and wash hands.
8. Record urine amount.

Note: To pass this skill, you will need to record a volume within 25 mL of the volume found by the evaluator.

The chemical component of urinalysis (U/A) can be done at point of care using a urine **dipstick** that is placed in a urine sample. The reagent pads on the dipstick change color when components being tested for are present. The dipstick can be read by comparing it to the color chart provided by the manufacturer.

Stool (fecal) samples are collected to test for disorders of the gastrointestinal (GI) system, including infections, cancers, and bleeding. **Fecal occult blood tests** (also called guaiac tests or guaiac smears) are a common test for occult (hidden) blood. Occult blood may be present if the patient has a GI disorder such as colorectal cancer or ulcerative colitis.

Stool samples may be collected in a large container placed inside the toilet. For smaller samples, the patient may use a scoop to place a small portion of feces in the collection container. The sample should be uncontaminated by urine.

Quick Review Question

9. To collect a midstream clean catch urine specimen, the nurse aide should:
   A) collect the first voided urine.
   B) clean the perianal region with antiseptic before collecting the specimen.
   C) attach a urinary collection bag over the genital area.
   D) ensure that the patient has fasted for at least 8 hours before specimen collection.

Glucose

Glucose levels in the blood can be tested at the point of care with small, portable glucose meters. A **lancet** is used to puncture the skin, and a small amount of blood is placed on the test strip. The meter then provides a readout of the glucose level. Important considerations for skin punctures include: ⌘ In adults, use the side of the middle or ring finger.

HELPFUL HINT

Normal blood glucose levels are 70 – 100

- In infants, puncture the heel.
- Puncture skin perpendicular to fingerprint lines.
- Never do a skin puncture at the site of a previous puncture or at a site that is bruised or swollen.
- Wipe away the first drop of blood before collecting the sample.
- Do not use povidone-iodine for skin puncture.

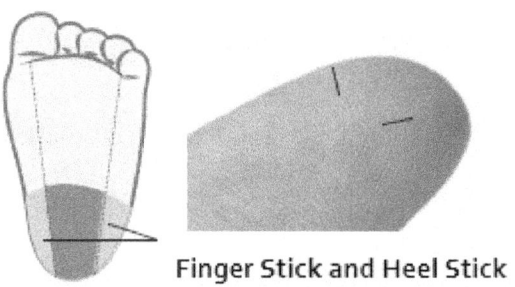

Finger Stick and Heel Stick

Quick Review Question

10. When testing glucose levels on an adult, the skin should be punctured on the:
    A) side of the middle finger.
    B) middle of the heel.
    C) palm of the nondominant hand.
    D) the big toe.

Wounds

A **wound** is a break in the skin. They may be caused by trauma, pressure, or underlying medical conditions (e.g., lack of blood flow). Wounds are classified based on the type of damage done to the skin.

- A **contusion** is a bruise caused by impact with a hard surface.
- An **abrasion** is scraping or rubbing of the skin.
- A **laceration** is a cut through the skin.
- A **skin tear** occurs when the top layer of the skin is pulled away.

An **ulcer** is a sore caused by the disintegration of the skin and underlying tissue.

Circulatory ulcers are caused by lack of blood flow to the affected area.

Diabetic foot ulcers are a common complication of diabetes.

Basic Nursing Skills

Pressure ulcers are caused by continued pressure on a localized area.

Some patients, including those who are over 65 years old, malnourished, or have underlying medical conditions, are at high risk of receiving wounds during medical care. Nurse aides must take preventive measures to avoid causing wounds. They will also provide care to maintain skin integrity and prevent wounds (particularly ulcers). General wound prevention guidelines are given below.

- Provide skin care to keep skin clean and dry.
- Apply moisturizer to dry areas.
- Use appropriate padding and lift devices to avoid skin tears when transferring and positioning patients.
- Reposition patients regularly (per care plan) to avoid pressure ulcers.
- Use pillows or specialized devices to prevent contact pressure on bony areas prone to pressure ulcers (e.g., heels, hips).
- Bathe gently with an appropriate cleanser and pat dry.
- Change linens and provide barriers as needed for incontinent patients.
- Be cautious when removing tape or dressings.
- Do not leave patients on equipment (e.g., bedpan, tubing) longer than necessary.
- Report changes in skin (e.g., redness, blisters) to nurse immediately.

Quick Review Question

11. A patient restrained in the prone position is at high risk for developing pressure ulcers on the:
    A) inner knee.
    B) back of knee.
    C) heel.
    D) hip.

Restraints

Restraints are devices that restrict the patient's movement. They may be used to manage patients with medical symptoms that pose a threat to the patient or caregivers. Use of restraints requires approval from a physician or a nurse (in an emergency only), and the details of restraint use must be included in the care plan.

> **HELPFUL HINT**
>
> Restraints should *never* be used to punish the patient or for the convenience of the nurse aide.

The nurse aide may be asked to monitor restrained patients. Patients should be checked at least every 15 minutes (per the care plan) to ensure that their airway, breathing, and circulation are not compromised. Every 2 hours, the patient should be released from the restraints so their personal and hygiene needs can be met (e.g., eating, elimination). Vital signs should also be taken. When reapplying restraints, the patient should be repositioned to avoid pressure ulcers or other position-related injuries.

Quick Review Question

12. A nurse aide has been asked to provide care for a patient who has just had wrist restraints removed. The nurse aide should do all of the following EXCEPT:
    A) tell the patient that if they cooperate the restraints will not be reapplied.
    B) help the patient with elimination needs.
    C) offer the patient fluids and food.
    D) take the patient's vital signs and assess the skin on the wrist.

ANSWER KEY

1. B) is correct. The nurse aide should respect the patient's privacy. If a patient is able to apply the drape, the aide should show them how to use it and allow them to undress and drape themselves.

2. C) is correct. In Fowler's position, the head of the bed is positioned between a 45° and 60° angle.

3. C) is correct. A temporal artery thermometer is used by sliding the thermometer across the forehead.

4. B) is correct. The carotid pulse is palpable lateral to the trachea.

5. D) is correct. The patient should be on their back (supine) so the nurse aide can see the rise and fall of their chest.

6. D) is correct. The stethoscope is placed over the brachial pulse (near the antecubital fossa) as the cuff is inflated and then slowly deflated.

7. D) is correct. 1 kilogram is equal to 2.2 pounds.

8. B) is correct. The abdomen is not a dependable location to measure pulse oximetry.

9. B) is correct. To collect a midstream clean catch urine sample, the nurse aide should clean the perianal region with antiseptic, allow the patient to void a small amount of urine, and then collect the urine sample.

10. A) is correct. On adults, a lancet should be used to puncture the skin on the side of the middle or ring finger to collect blood for testing.

11. C) is correct. Patients in a prone position will experience pressure on their heels as their feet rest on the mattress.

12. A) is correct. The nurse aide does not control when restraints are applied and should not use the threat of restraints to gain the patient's cooperation.

Safety and Infection Control

Infection Control

Infection Cycle and the Chain of Infection

The goal of **infection control** is to intervene in the chain of infection at the point where infection is most likely to occur in order to prevent its spread. **Infection** occurs when an organism establishes an opportunistic relationship with a host. Infections can be caused by many different infectious agents.

Bacteria are single-celled prokaryotic organisms that are responsible for many common infections such as strep throat, urinary tract infections, and many food-borne illnesses.

Viruses are composed of a nucleic acid (DNA or RNA) wrapped in a protein capsid. They invade host cells and hijack cell machinery to reproduce. Viral infections include the common cold, influenza, and human immunodeficiency virus (HIV).

Protozoa are single-celled eukaryotic organisms. Protozoan infections include giardia (an intestinal infection) and African sleeping sickness.

Fungi are a group of eukaryotic organisms that include yeasts, molds, and mushrooms. Common fungal infections are athlete's foot, ringworm, and oral and vaginal yeast infections.

Parasitic diseases are caused by parasites that live in or on the human body and use its resources. Common human parasites include worms (e.g., tapeworms), flukes, and ectoparasites like lice and ticks, which live on the outside of the body.

Infections travel from person to person via the **chain of infection**. The chain starts with a causative organism (e.g., a bacteria or virus). The organism needs a **reservoir**, or place to live. The reservoir may be biological (e.g., people or animals), or it may be environmental. For example, in a medical office, equipment and office surfaces may act as reservoirs. In order to spread, the

> **HELPFUL HINT**
>
> Infectious disease precautions are categorized based on how the disease is transmitted. For example, droplet precautions require only a surgical mask, but airborne precautions require an N-95 respirator to prevent transmission.

infectious agent needs a way to exit the reservoir, such as being expelled as droplets during a sneeze.

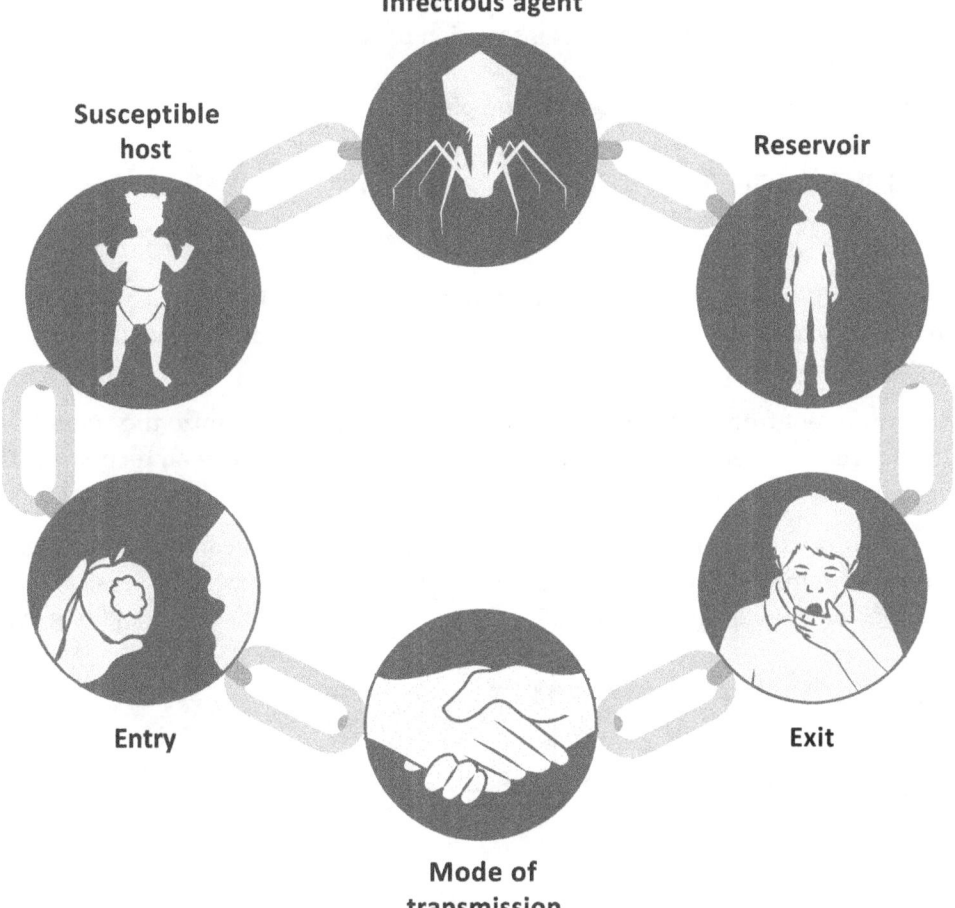

For the infection chain to continue, the infectious agent needs to encounter a susceptible **host**—a person who can become infected. Finally, the infectious agent needs a way to enter the host, such as through inhalation or drinking contaminated water. Infections may be transmitted to hosts via several modes of transmission.

Direct contact is transmission from one infected person to another during physical contact with blood or other body fluids (e.g., transmission of herpes during sexual intercourse).

Indirect contact is transmission of the disease through a nonbiological reservoir (e.g., drinking water contaminated with giardia).

Droplets are infectious agents trapped in moisture that are expelled when an infected person sneezes or coughs. They can enter the respiratory system of other people and cause infection (e.g., transmission of influenza when an infected person sneezes).

Some droplets are light enough to remain **airborne**, meaning people may inhale infectious agents from the air long after the initial cough or sneeze (e.g., measles, which can live in airborne droplets for up to two hours).

Some diseases are carried by organisms called **vectors** that spread the disease; the infection does not require direct physical contact between people (e.g., mosquitoes carrying malaria).

> **Quick Review Question**
>
> 1. Which of the following is an example of transmission of an infectious agent through direct contact?
>   A) kissing an infected person
>   B) inhaling droplets from a sneezing infected person
>   C) eating contaminated food
>   D) inhaling microorganisms in the air

Asepsis

Asepsis is the absence of infectious organisms, and **medical asepsis** is the practice of destroying infectious agents outside the body to prevent the spread of disease. An object that has had all infectious agents removed or destroyed is **sterile**.

Medical asepsis is different from **clean technique**, which also aims to minimize the spread of infectious agents but does not require sterilization. Wearing gloves is an example of clean technique; the gloves are not sterile, but they provide a barrier that prevents the spread of infection from patient to provider.

The most important tool used for medical asepsis is handwashing. **Aseptic handwashing** is a specific technique intended to remove all infectious agents from the hands and wrists. Aseptic handwashing should be performed whenever the nurse aide is going to interact with a sterile field (e.g., when applying a sterile dressing).

Skills Evaluation: Handwashing

1. Turn on water.
2. Wet hands and wrists.
3. Apply soap.
4. Lather fingers, hands, and wrists for 20 seconds. (Keep hands lower than elbows and fingers down.)
5. Clean fingernails on opposite palm.
6. Rinse fingers, hands, and wrists. (Keep hands lower than elbows and fingers down.)
7. Use clean towel to dry hands and dispose of towel.
8. Use clean towel or foot control to turn off faucet.

> **HELPFUL HINT**
>
> Clean or sterile surfaces become contaminated when they come in contact with pathogens.

Medical asepsis also includes the removal of infectious agents from equipment and other surfaces. This process has three levels.

Cleaning removes dirt and some infectious agents.

Disinfection kills all pathogens except bacterial spores. Most surfaces in health care settings are disinfected using chemical agents such as alcohol or chlorine bleach.

Safety and Infection Control

Sterilization kills all infectious agents, including bacterial spores. Medical equipment is sterilized using heat or chemicals (e.g., ethylene oxide).

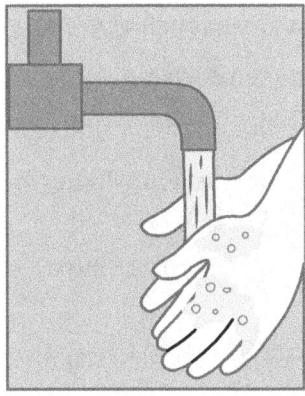

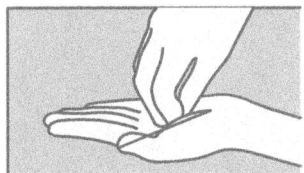

Fingernails

Surgical asepsis is the practice of removing all infectious pathogens from all equipment involved in invasive procedures. Nurse aides may be asked to help sterilize equipment and may also be required to do a surgical scrub if participating in an invasive procedure. A **sterile field** is a work area free of contaminants.

Quick Review Question

2. A surface is disinfected after it has been:
    A) cleaned with chlorine bleach.
    B) washed with soap and water.
    C) covered with a drape sheet.
    D) allowed to sit unused for 24 hours.

Personal Protective Equipment

In addition to handwashing, equipment can be used to prevent the spread of infection. **Personal protective equipment (PPE)** is any item necessary for the prevention of microorganism transmission. PPE includes gloves, gowns, goggles, eye shields, and masks. Some general guidelines for using PPE are given below.

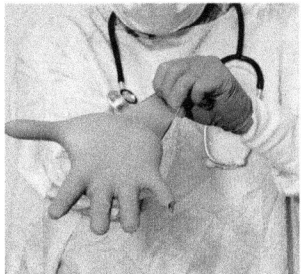

Safety and Infection Control

- Wear gloves when the hands may contact bodily fluids, broken skin, or contaminated surfaces.
- Change contaminated gloves before touching a clean body site or clean equipment.
- Gloves must be discarded between each patient.
- The outside of gloves is contaminated; the inside of gloves is clean.
- Masks are used both to protect medical providers from splashes and to protect patients from infectious agents carried by the provider.
- Goggles and face shields are worn to protect the eyes, mouth, and nose from body fluid splashes.
- The order for putting on PPE is 1) gown, 2) mask, 3) goggles/face shield, 4) gloves.
- Remove all PPE except respirators before leaving the patient's room.
- Wash hands after removing PPE.

Skills Evaluation: Donning and Removing Gown and Gloves

1. Unfold gown and put arms through sleeves.
2. Fasten gown at neck and then at waist.
3. Put on gloves so that gloves cover gown cuff.
4. Remove gloves:

    Use one gloved hand to grasp the other glove at the palm and remove.

    Slide ungloved fingers under the remaining glove cuff, and remove while turning glove inside out.

    Dispose of gloves.

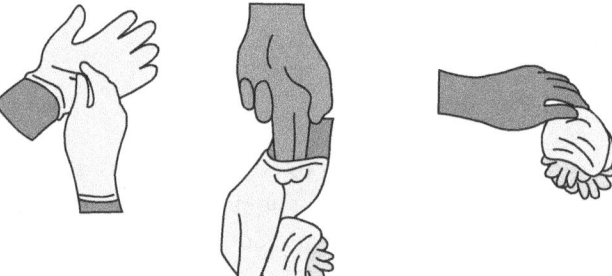

5. Untie and remove gown without touching contaminated area of gown.
6. Dispose of gown.
7. Wash hands.

Quick Review Question

3. Which of the following statements about PPE is NOT correct?
    A) Hands do not need to be washed before putting on gloves.
    B) A face shield is worn when body fluid splashes are likely.
    C) Fluid-resistant gowns should be removed after leaving a patient's room.
    D) PPE devices include gloves, gowns, eye shields, and masks.

Standard Precautions and Blood Borne Pathogen Standards

Standard precautions (also called universal precautions) are based on the assumption that all patients are infected with microorganisms, whether or not there are symptoms or a diagnosis. Standard precautions decrease the risk of transmission of microorganisms from blood and other body fluids. The standards apply to contact with blood, all body fluids, secretions, and excretions (except sweat), non-intact skin, and mucous membranes.

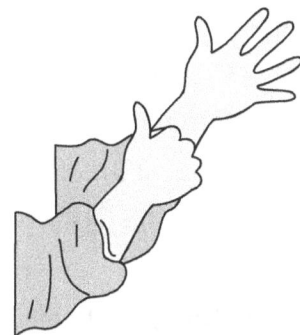

This set of principles is used by all health care workers who have direct or indirect contact with patients. When working with patients and specimens, the nurse aide should always follow these standard precautions:

- Assume that all patients are carrying a microorganism.
- Use appropriate PPE.
- Practice hand hygiene.
- Follow needle-stick prevention policies.
- Clean and disinfect surfaces after each patient.
- Use disposable barriers to protect surfaces that are hard to disinfect.

Additional precautions may be needed for patients with known infections. These precautions are based on the transmission route for the infection.

Airborne precautions:

- Wear N-95 respirator mask; place on before entering the room and keep on until after leaving the room.

> **HELPFUL HINT**
>
> Hand hygiene: Use soap and water when hands are visibly soiled. Antimicrobial foam or gel may be used if hands are not visibly soiled.

- Place N-95 or surgical mask on patient during transport.
- Patient may be placed in a private room with a negative-pressure air system with the door kept closed.

Droplet precautions:

- Place patient in a private room; the door may remain open.
- Wear appropriate PPE within 3 feet of patient.
- Wash hands with antimicrobial soap after removing gloves and mask and before leaving the patient's room.
- Place surgical mask on patient during transport.

Contact precautions:

- Place the patient in a private room; the door may remain open.
- Wear gloves.
- Change gloves after touching infected materials.
- Remove gloves before leaving patient's room.
- Wear gown; remove before leaving patient's room.
- Use patient-dedicated equipment if possible; clean and disinfect community equipment between patients.

Quick Review Question

4. The use of standard precautions is NOT required for contact with:
   A) blood.
   B) urine.
   C) sweat.
   D) vomit.

Biohazard Disposal and Regulated Waste

Regulated medical waste (RMW) (also called biohazardous waste) is any waste that is or may be contaminated with infectious materials, including blood, secretions, and excretions. Regulated medical waste must be handled carefully to prevent the possibility of an exposure incident. The disposal of RMW is governed by federal, state, and local regulations that vary by location. Some general waste disposal guidelines are given below.

Sharps should be disposed of in a **biohazard sharps container**. The term "sharps" refers to needles, lancets, blood tubes, capillary tubes, razor blades, suturing needles, hypodermic needles, and microscope slides and coverslips.

Blood and body fluids, such as urine, sputum, semen, amniotic fluid, and cerebrospinal fluid, can be disposed of in a drain, toilet, or utility sink. State and local regulations may limit the amount of fluid that can be disposed of into the sewage system.

Feces should be flushed in a toilet.

Bandages, dressing gauzes, and gloves with small amounts of RMW can be put in regular garbage disposal cans.

Dirty linen should be put in a separate receptacle; if very soiled by blood or infectious material, it should be put in a biohazard bag.

Chemicals should be stored and disposed of according to the information in the **safety data sheets (SDSs)**, which are provided by the manufacturer.

Spill kits are a collection of substances and PPE that assist in cleaning and containing infectious agents or chemical agents after a spill. Spill kits may be general purpose, or they may be tailored to a specific substance (e.g., mercury or body fluids).

> **Quick Review Question**
>
> 5. A patient diagnosed with C. diff has soiled the bed, and the nurse aide is stripping the bed. The nurse aide should:
>   A) throw the linens in the trash can.
>   B) place the linens in a red biohazard bag.
>   C) place the soiled linens in a regular dirty linen bag.
>   D) rinse the soiled linens before placing them in a soiled linen bag.

Emergency Response

Emergency Care

A **medical emergency** is an unexpected, life-threatening event. It can occur at any time, so it is important to be prepared and understand what to do. A nurse aide's role is to stay calm and follow the office's emergency management policy and protocol. The more prepared the nurse aide is for an emergency, the better the outcome will be for the patient. Knowing how to recognize common emergency situations and what to do can help ensure that the patient remains safe and the event does not escalate.

> **HELPFUL HINT**
> It is important that the nurse aide does not attempt to diagnose or independently treat any issues. If the nurse aide believes a patient has symptoms requiring urgent assessment or treatment, the appropriate medical provider should be notified immediately.

Some key points for the nurse aide to remember during an emergency are:

- Secure the scene and do not panic.
- Relocate nearby visitors and patients.
- Work with other members of the healthcare team to ensure that all necessary equipment is available.

Know the location of the crash cart.

Maintain cardiopulmonary resuscitation (CPR) certification and follow training.

Do not attempt any intervention without the proper training.

Be observant; the nurse aide may need to provide information about the event.

Remember to complete all applicable documentation regarding the emergency.

Anaphylactic Shock

> **HELPFUL HINT**
> Many patients with allergies carry an EpiPen, which provides a premeasured dose of epinephrine for injection.

Anaphylactic shock (or anaphylaxis) is a life-threatening, severe allergic reaction that causes widening of blood vessels and constriction of airways in the lungs. The most common causes of anaphylactic shock are food allergens, medications, and insect venom. Symptoms of anaphylactic shock include:

- respiratory distress (can be severe)
- swelling (edema) in face, lips, or tongue
- skin pallor or flushing
- low blood pressure
- dizziness or fainting
- altered mental status

Anaphylactic shock is treated with an epinephrine injection. The provider may choose to transfer the patient to an emergency department for further observation or if treatment is ineffective.

Bleeding

There are three types of bleeding: arterial, venous, and capillary.

Arterial bleeding occurs when an artery is damaged. Because arteries carry high volumes of blood at high pressure, arterial bleeding can be life threatening and requires immediate intervention to prevent low blood pressure and other problems related to decrease in blood volume.

Arterial blood is bright red and "spurts" due to the pressure of the heart pumping. The blood is often moving too quickly for clotting to occur.

Venous bleeding occurs when a vein is damaged. Veins carry high volumes of blood, but they do not supply the same pressure as arteries, so although venous bleeding may be heavy, it is slower than arterial bleeding. The blood is also darker in color because it is deoxygenated.

Capillary bleeding occurs when the small blood vessels that create the network between veins and arteries are damaged. Capillary bleeding is often seen in wound beds or with skin abrasions. Bleeding from the capillaries is usually controlled easily.

The treatment for all types of bleeding is to apply direct pressure to the site.

Maintain standard precautions, including wearing gloves.

Place the patient in a prone position.

Apply pressure using sterile gauze. Pressure may be applied for up to 20 minutes depending on the type of bleed. If the bleed is arterial, pressure may be applied above the site of the bleeding (only if directed by the provider).

Assist with cleaning and dressing the wound once the bleeding has stopped.

Cardiac and Respiratory Arrest

Cardiopulmonary (cardiac) arrest occurs when the heart stops beating, which causes blood flow to stop. The patient will have no pulse and either will not be breathing or will display labored breathing (agonal gasps). Immediately start cardiopulmonary resuscitation (CPR) for any patient in arrest.

Respiratory arrest occurs when breathing stops or is no longer effective at meeting the body's oxygen needs. Respiratory arrest often occurs with cardiac arrest but can occur alone as well. It will eventually lead to cardiac arrest.

Both cardiac and respiratory arrest are life-threatening conditions that require immediate treatment to preserve life and tissue function. The nurse aide should follow these steps:

Get help and contact 911.

Assess the patient and check for pulse (for no longer than five seconds). If the patient has a pulse, perform rescue breathing. If the patient has no pulse, begin performing CPR.

Rescue breathing:

Use the head tilt–chin lift method to assess the airway.

Ensure the patient's airway is clear.

If an obstruction is visible, attempt to clear it. However, be careful to not obstruct the airway by pushing the object in deeper.

Provide breaths at a rate of 10 to 12 breaths a minute.

CPR:

Perform chest compressions at a rate of 30 compressions to two breaths for a single rescuer, with a goal of 100 compressions a minute.

Compressions should be 2 inches in depth.

Allow full chest recoil.

Use the head tilt–chin lift method to assess the airway after the first 30 compressions.

Use the automated external defibrillator (AED) as necessary.

Cerebrovascular Accident (CVA)

> **HELPFUL HINT**
> Do not remove blood-soaked dressings, as this will interrupt the clotting process. Instead add gauze as necessary.

A **cerebrovascular accident (CVA)**, or **stroke**, occurs when the blood supply to the brain is disrupted due to damage in the brain's blood vessels. A **hemorrhagic stroke** occurs when a vessel ruptures in the brain. The blood that accumulates damages brain Tissue and causes neurological impairment. An **ischemic stroke** occurs when arteries in the brain are blocked, leading to ischemia (reduced blood flow) and damage to brain tissue.

During a cerebrovascular event or stroke, response time is critical—the longer the CVA is untreated, the more damage will be done to the brain. The nurse aide should be able to recognize the symptoms of a stroke and communicate these to the provider. Patients may present with:

- unilateral face drooping
- arm weakness
- speech difficulty
- confusion
- severe headache

> **HELPFUL HINT**
> Choking is the most common cause of respiratory distress in pediatric patients.

Foreign Body Obstruction

Choking is caused by a foreign body obstructing the airway. Unaddressed choking will lead to loss of consciousness and cardiac arrest. If a patient begins choking, the nurse aide should alert the nearest provider and attempt to dislodge the obstruction until a provider is available. Never perform a blind sweep, as this may lodge the object farther in the airway.

If the patient is conscious, use the **Heimlich maneuver** or abdominal thrusts to dislodge the object. For an infant with an obstructed airway, the nurse aide should switch between five back slaps and five abdominal thrusts.

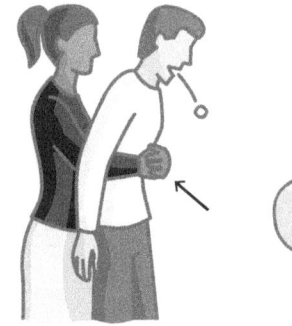
Heimlich maneuver

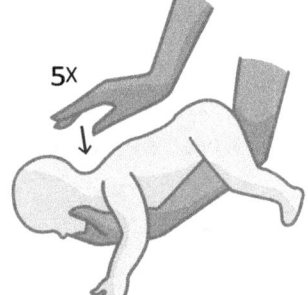
Back slaps

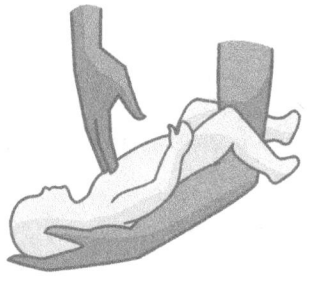
Abdominal thrusts in infant

Seizures

A **seizure** is caused by abnormal electrical discharges in the cortical gray matter of the brain; the discharges interrupt normal brain function. **Epilepsy** is a condition characterized by recurrent seizures.

Tonic-clonic seizures (a type of convulsive seizure) start with a tonic (contracted) state in which the patient stiffens and loses consciousness; this phase usually lasts less than one minute. The tonic phase is followed by the clonic phase, in which the patient's muscles rapidly contract and relax. The clonic phase can last up to several minutes.

During a seizure, the nurse aide should act to secure the safety of the patient:

- Remove any objects that might cause injury.
- Loosen tight clothing.
- Never restrain a seizing patient.
- Do not place anything in the patient's mouth.
- If needed, place the patient in the recovery position (on their side).

- Post-seizure patients are usually lethargic; allow recovery time.
- Ensure that the physician is aware of the situation.

Syncope

Syncope (fainting) is temporary partial or full loss of consciousness caused by decreased circulation of blood to the brain. Often syncope is in response to temperature changes, low blood pressure, fear or surprise, or low blood sugar. Symptoms that may precede an episode include flushing, dizziness, sweating, weakness, and paleness.

If the patient presents with syncopal symptoms, the nurse aide should make sure they are not in danger of falling by having them sit or lie down. The provider will conduct a full examination.

Quick Review Question

6. A patient is having a tonic-clonic seizure. What should the nurse aide do first?
   A) Call 911.
   B) Restrain the patient.
   C) Take the patient's vital signs.
   D) Provide a safe environment.

Emergency Equipment

It is important that an office have a crash cart or area where emergency equipment is easily accessible. Nurse aides should be familiar with the location of emergency equipment and how it is used. The nurse aide may be asked to retrieve or use supplies from the crash cart. The table below provides a list of common medical equipment that may be needed in an emergency.

> **HELPFUL HINT**
> Water should never be used to put out electrical, grease, or chemical fires. The appropriate fire extinguisher should be used instead.

Table 3.1. Common Emergency Medical Equipment

Equipment	Use
AED	restarts normal cardiac rhythm in patients with specific dysrhythmias
Portable oxygen tank	provides oxygen to patients with low oxygen saturation
Suction equipment	clears airways
Endotracheal tubes	opens airways and provides mechanical ventilation
CPR mask	covers patient's mouth during CPR
Bag-valve mask (this may have an oxygen hookup)	provides ventilation during cardiac or respiratory arrest

Table 3.1. Common Emergency Medical Equipment

Equipment	Use
Emergency medications	epinephrine: anaphylactic shock and cardiac arrest atropine: slow heart rate (bradycardia) sodium bicarb: high acid levels in blood and some types of overdoses activated charcoal: some poisonings ipecac: to induce vomiting aspirin: for patients experiencing acute coronary symptoms
IV supplies	for administration of fluids and medications
Dressings	for controlling bleeding and dressing wounds
PPE including gowns, gloves, surgical masks, and N-95 respirators	to prevent spread of infections

Quick Review Question

7. A medical provider is caring for a patient in cardiac arrest. The nurse aide should anticipate that the provider may ask for:
   A) dressings.
   B) aspirin.
   C) a bag-valve mask.
   D) an N-95 respirator.

Fire and Electrical Safety

Although rare, fires in medical offices do occur. The nurse aide should be aware of certain fire safety measures:

- Keep open spaces free of clutter.
- Know the locations of fire exits, alarms, and extinguishers.
- Participate in fire drills and know the evacuation plan of the health care facility.
- Do not use the elevator when a fire occurs.
- Turn off oxygen in the vicinity of a fire.
- Unplug electrical equipment that is malfunctioning or is near a fire.

Before use, electrical equipment should be inspected for defects and safety by checking three-pronged outlets and reading warning labels. Any electrical cords that are exposed, damaged, or frayed should be discarded, and circuits should not be overloaded. Safety measures include:

Never run electrical wiring under carpets.

Do not pull a plug by yanking the cord.

Never use electrical appliances near bathtubs, sinks, or other water sources

Disconnect plugs from the outlet before cleaning appliances or equipment.

Quick Review Question

8. The nurse aide should be prepared to perform all the following safety measures EXCEPT:
    A) participate in fire drills.
    B) remove candles from patient rooms.
    C) unplug malfunctioning equipment.
    D) use a fire extinguisher.

ANSWER KEY

1. A) is correct. Direct contact is the transmission of infectious agents through physical contact between two people, such as kissing.

2. A) is correct. Chlorine bleach is a disinfectant that will kill most pathogens.

3. C) is correct. Fluid-resistant gowns should be removed BEFORE leaving the patient's room to prevent spread of infection into the hallway.

4. C) is correct. Standard precautions are recommended whenever the nurse aide comes in contact with blood or body fluids that could transmit blood-borne pathogens. Blood-borne pathogens cannot be transmitted via sweat.

5. B) is correct. *C. diff* is highly contagious, and soiled linens require special handling. The nurse aide should place all linens in a red biohazard bag and put the bag in the designated area for biohazard bags in the soiled utility area.

6. D) is correct. Safety is the top priority during seizure activity, so the nurse aide should remove any objects in the immediate area that may cause the patient harm.

7. C) is correct. The patient in cardiac arrest requires CPR, and a bag-valve mask is used to deliver breaths during CPR.

8. B) is correct. The nurse aide should not take a patient's personal property. If the nurse aide has concerns about a patient's safety, they should alert the nurse.

Psychosocial Care Skills

Emotional, Spiritual, and Cultural Needs

Abraham Maslow's **hierarchy of needs** describes the needs that drive people's behavior. According to Maslow, as each stage is achieved, a person is encouraged to move to the next stage. The stages are often depicted as a pyramid: a person must meet the needs at the bottom of the pyramid before they can address needs at higher levels.

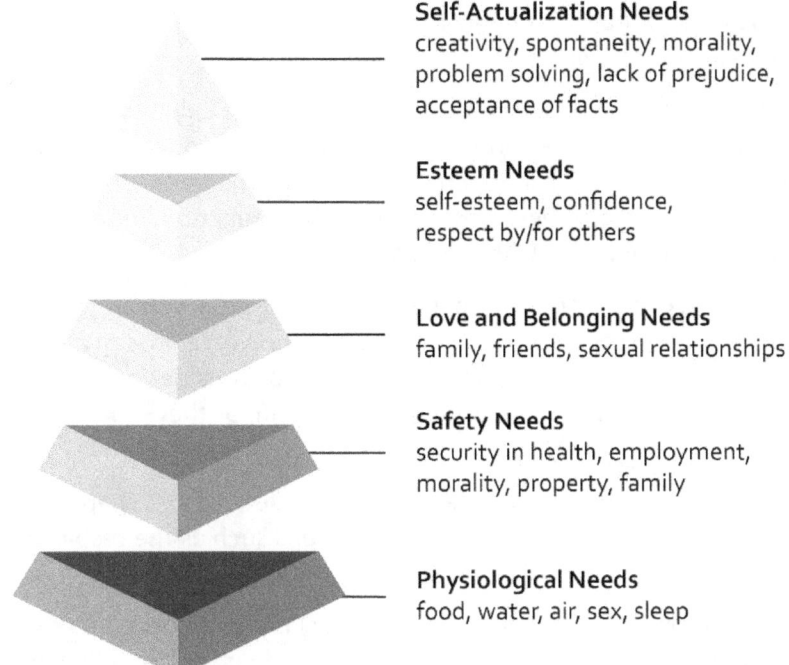

Self-Actualization Needs
creativity, spontaneity, morality, problem solving, lack of prejudice, acceptance of facts

Esteem Needs
self-esteem, confidence, respect by/for others

Love and Belonging Needs
family, friends, sexual relationships

Safety Needs
security in health, employment, morality, property, family

Physiological Needs
food, water, air, sex, sleep

Patients will also have needs specific to their culture and spirituality. For example, patients may choose not to eat certain foods, or they may wish to attend religious services. These needs may be included in the care plan, or the patient may express them to the nurse aide. The nurse aide should respect patients' cultural and spiritual needs and should not ignore, judge, or challenge them.

> **HELPFUL HINT**
> If the patient's request interferes with care or the patient has needs the nurse aide cannot meet, the nurse aide should alert the nurse.

> **HELPFUL HINT**
> Altered behavior may be caused by a wide range of medical conditions, including hypoglycemia, stroke, head injury, and hypoxia (low oxygen). Sudden changes in a patient's behavior or mental status should always be reported to the nurse so the patient can be further assessed.

Quick Review Question

1. A Muslim patient refuses to eat their lunch because it contains pork. The nurse aid should:
    A) tell the patient to only eat the foods that do not contain pork.
    B) take the food tray from the patient and tell them they will get a different meal at dinner.
    C) explain to the patient that eating protein is important for health.
    D) alert the nurse that the patient needs to be brought a halal lunch.

Mental Health Needs

Mental Health Disorders

The nurse aide should be able to recognize behaviors related to mental health disorders and be prepared to care for patients with altered behavior or mental status.

Delirium is a temporary cognitive change from baseline. The patient exhibits confusion and disorientation with a decreased ability to focus or hold attention. **Dementia** is a broad term for progressive, cognitively debilitating symptoms that interfere with independent functioning. Patients may show decline in one or more cognitive domains, including language, memory, executive function, motor skills, or social cognition. The most common cause of dementia is **Alzheimer's disease**.

A **situational crisis** is an acute change or event in a patient's life that may lead to feelings of anxiety, fear, depression, or other mental or emotional illness concerns (e.g., divorce, loss of a family member). **Suicidal ideation** is characterized by feelings or thoughts of attempting or considering suicide. Patients exhibiting suicidal ideation may have vague thoughts without a distinct plan, or they may have a specific plan and the means to carry it out.

Anxiety refers to feelings of fear, apprehension, and worry. Anxiety can be characterized as mild, moderate, or severe (panic). Anxiety will impact other functions such as the respiratory, cardiac, and gastrointestinal systems.

Bipolar disorder (formerly known as manic-depressive illness) is characterized by extreme shifts between mania and depression. **Mania** is a state of high energy, increased activity, and feelings of elation and immortality. **Depression** is a mood disorder characterized by feelings of sadness and hopelessness.

Quick Review Question

2. A patient undergoing rehabilitation after a stroke tells the nurse aide that he would "rather die than keep living like this." The nurse aide should:
    A) encourage the patient not to give up on his rehabilitation program.
    B) alert the nurse that the patient has expressed suicidal ideation.
    C) ignore the patient's statement and continue his rehabilitation.
    D) ask the patient why he is depressed.

Caring for Patients with Altered Behavioral or Mental Status

When communicating with patients with altered behavior or mental status, the nurse aide should always respect the patient and treat them with dignity and consideration. Speak in a slow, clear voice, and do not judge the patient or speak harshly. (See chapter 5 for more information on patient communication.)

Patients with dementia, delirium, or confusion require special care to meet their mental health needs. Some guidelines for caring for these patients are below.

- Do not challenge or affirm patients with delusions or hallucinations. Instead, redirect the conversation toward what is real.
- Do not argue with patients engaged in altered behavior (e.g., wandering, repetitive actions). Instead, keep them safe as they engage in these behaviors, and alert the nurse if intervention is needed.
- Follow routines and do not make changes to the environment.
- Use memory aids as described in the care plan.
- Explain procedures with simple, step-by-step instructions.
- Ensure the patient has access to items, activities, and people they enjoy or find soothing.

Patients with mental health disorders may become angry or violent. Mild aggression can be handled by the nurse aide, who can help address the cause, provide a soothing environment, or distract the patient. The nurse aide may also firmly ask the patient to stop the behavior. If the patient is abusive or violent, the nurse aide should prioritize their own safety and not try to manage the patient on their own. They may leave the room and then alert the nurse and security so they can safely manage the patient.

Quick Review Question

3. A nurse aide is feeding a patient with Alzheimer's who tells the nurse aide that his wife is in the room. The nurse aide knows that the patient's wife recently died. The nurse aide should:
    A) ask the patient if he likes his meal and wants to keep eating.
    B) gently remind the patient that his wife is dead.
    C) alert the nurse that the patient is experiencing psychosis.
    D) ask the patient what his wife is saying.

ANSWER KEY

1. D) is correct. The nurse aide should respect the patient's religious needs. They should alert the nurse that the patient has requested a halal diet (which meets Muslim dietary restrictions). The patient can then be brought a new lunch, and the nurse can update the patient's care plan.

2. B) is correct. When a patient expresses suicidal thoughts, the nurse aide should alert the nurse as soon as possible so that the patient can receive the appropriate care.

3. A) is correct. Confusion is normal in patients with Alzheimer's. The nurse aide should not reinforce or challenge the patient's delusions and instead should focus the patient's attention on real, concrete behaviors.

Role of the Nurse Aide

Communication can be verbal or nonverbal. **Verbal communication** refers to words that are spoken or written. Guidelines for verbal communication are given in Table 5.1.

Table 5.1. Dos and Don'ts of Patient Communication

Do	Don't
Introduce yourself and use the patient's name. Speak directly to the patient when possible. Speak slowly and clearly. Show empathy for the patient. Be silent when appropriate to allow patients time to think and process emotions.	Use medical jargon. Threaten or intimidate the patient. Lie or provide false hope. Interrupt the patient. Show frustration or anger. Make judgmental statements.

Nonverbal communication includes all the physical aspects of communication, including posture, facial expression, and eye contact. Nurse aides should strive to keep their nonverbal communication professional and appropriate by:

- maintaining good posture (e.g., not slouching on a desk).
- keeping a polite facial expression when dealing with patients and the health care team.
- respecting other people's personal boundaries (e.g., not touching patients without their consent).
- maintaining eye contact when speaking with patients and the health care team.
- not using rude or inappropriate hand gestures.

Special communication techniques may be needed when working with diverse populations. Some of these guidelines are given in Table 5.2.

Table 5.2. Communicating with Diverse Populations

Population	Communication Techniques
Blind or low vision	Announce when you enter or leave the room. Address the patient by name. Describe the layout of the room. Narrate your actions.
Deaf or hard of hearing	Speak slowly and clearly. Allow the patient to see your face while you speak. Provide written materials. Use a sign language interpreter when needed.
Geriatric	Adjust language for confused or cognitively impaired patients. Rely on family members or caregivers as needed.
Pediatric	Move to patient's eye level. Use simple language. Explain exam procedures before you start. Allow patient to hold blunt, safe instruments.
Seriously or terminally ill	Respond promptly and allow patients any needed extra time. Be direct but kind. Do not offer false hope or make unfulfillable promises.
Intellectually disabled	Match the patient's level of vocabulary and sentence complexity. Speak directly to the patient.
Illiterate	Notice when patients do not read materials. Read or explain important documents.
Non-English speaking	Have materials available in multiple languages. Use an interpreter when needed.

Quick Review Question

1. When questioning a patient through an interpreter, questions should be directed toward:
   A) the interpreter.
   B) the nurse.
   C) the patient's family.
   D) the patient.

Client Rights

Many different sets of **client rights** have been described by lawmakers and professional organizations. The two sets of client rights the nurse aide should be familiar with come from the American Hospital Association (AHA) and the Omnibus Budget Reconciliation Act of 1987 (OBRA).

The AHA formulated the **Patient's Bill of Rights** in 1973. This document outlines a patient's right to:
- receive respectful, considerate, and appropriate care.
- expect privacy and confidentiality.
- consult the physician of his or her choice.
- make decisions regarding health care.
- refuse treatment.
- receive continuity of care.
- obtain copies of his or her medical record.
- participate or refuse to participate in research.
- receive all information regarding diagnosis, treatment, and prognosis.
- make informed decisions related to health care.

In 2003, the AHA created the **Patient Care Partnership**. This brochure explains to patients what to expect during their hospital stay and outlines the hospital's responsibilities. The Patient Care Partnership outlines six key rights for all patients:
- high-quality hospital care
- clean and safe environment
- involvement in care
- protection of privacy
- help when leaving the hospital
- help with billing claims

The Omnibus Budget Reconciliation Act of 1987 (OBRA) outlines the rights held by residents of nursing centers. These are similar to those listed in the Patient Care Partnership and include the right to:

- be treated with dignity and respect.
- access records of care.
- refuse care.
- maintain privacy and confidentiality.
- have personal items and engage in personal activities and interests.

> **HELPFUL HINT**
> Nurse aides have an ethical (and sometimes legal) duty to report signs of child or elder abuse.

Quick Review Question

2. Patients have the right to do all of the following EXCEPT:
   A) refuse care.
   B) choose their nurse.
   C) see their medical record.
   D) expect privacy.

Legal and Ethical Behavior

Ethics

Ethics are moral principles, values, and duties. Whereas laws are enforceable regulations set by the government, ethics are moral guidelines set and formally or informally enforced by peers, the community, and professional organizations. The following guidelines can help guide the ethical conduct of the nurse aide: ⌘ work within the nurse aide scope of practice ⌘ prioritize the patient's needs over your own ⌘ do not perform any act that will harm the patient ⌘ follow the directions of the nurse ⌘ protect patients' privacy and confidentiality ⌘ report errors immediately

Quick Review Question

3. A nurse aide sees a patient steal money from a visitor's purse. The nurse aide should:
   A) alert the nurse that a patient has stolen money.
   B) confront the patient and demand they return the money.
   C) tell the visitor that a patient stole their money.
   D) do nothing and let the visitor address the issue.

Legal Issues

A **tort** is a wrongful civil act. Tort laws involve the accidental or intentional harm to a person or property that results from the wrongdoing of a person or persons. **Negligence** is a type of tort, defined as failure to offer an acceptable standard of care that is comparable to what a competent health care worker would provide in a similar situation. There are four types of negligence:

Nonfeasance: a willful failure to act when required

Misfeasance: the incorrect or improper performance of a lawful action.

Malfeasance: a willful and intentional action that causes harm.

Malpractice: a professional's failure to properly execute their duties.

Role of the Nurse Aide

Intentional torts are committed when a person purposefully causes harm to another. Some examples include:

- battery: harmful or offensive contact with another person
- assault: an attempted battery in which there was threat of injury, but no injury occurred
- slander: saying something false about someone that causes damage to their reputation
- libel: writing something false about someone that causes damage to their reputation

Consent for various medical services and health care involves verbal or written permission from the patient. Expressed consent must be **informed**, which requires a trained health care worker explaining the necessary information to the patient so he or she can make an educated decision. **Implied consent** is usually made in life-threatening circumstances and medical emergencies based on the assumption that the patient would consent to lifesaving care. It can also refer to consent suggested by a patient's actions (e.g., extending their arm to have blood drawn).

Quick Review Question

4. A patient opening their mouth so the nurse aide can use an oral thermometer is an example of:
   A) informed consent.
   B) implied consent.
   C) battery.
   D) malpractice.

Members of the Health Care Team

Nurse Aide Scope of Practice

The nurse aide assists the nurse and performs tasks assigned to them by a nurse. The nurse aide may only perform tasks designated to them by appropriate personnel and cannot decide what care a patient needs. The care provided by the nurse aide may include:

assisting patients with activities of daily living

collecting patient specimens for testing

caring for wounds

assisting with rehabilitation exercises

any other tasks requested by a nurse for which the nurse aide has been properly trained

The nurse aide should NEVER:

perform a task they have not been properly trained for

provide care that has not been requested by a nurse

alter a patient's care plan

> **HELPFUL HINT**
> Patients have a right to choose or refuse care, and providing care without consent may be considered battery.

Quick Review Question

5. Which of the following actions falls within the nurse aide's scope of practice?
   A) obtaining a stool sample
   B) prescribing medications
   C) triaging patients in the waiting room
   D) educating patients at discharge

Other Members of the Healthcare Team

The nurse aide will work with a variety of health care team members, each of whom performs a specific set of duties. Nurse aides should be familiar with the roles and skills of other health care team members.

certified medical assistant (CMA): A CMA has general administrative office skills and basic nursing skills. They obtain basic medical history and information from patients, take vital signs, collect and test specimens, and assist providers with procedures.

licensed practical nurse (LPN): An LPN is a one-year nurse trained in patient care and licensed by the state.

registered nurse (RN): An RN is a two- or four-year nurse trained in patient care and licensed by the state.

nurse practitioner (NP): An NP is an RN with advanced training to diagnose and treat patients in the health care environment.

clinical nurse specialist (CNS): A CNS has advanced education and training in a specialized field, such as psychiatric care, women's health, or critical care. They can make diagnoses, develop treatment plans, and provide care.

physician assistant (PA): A PA is trained to practice medicine under the supervision of a physician.

physician: Physicians have completed a doctor of medicine (MD) degree. They can diagnose conditions, order procedures, treat patients, and write medication prescriptions for illnesses.

emergency medical technician (EMT): An EMT is trained in the administration of emergency care and transportation of patients to the medical facility.

phlebotomist: Also called an accessioning technician, a phlebotomist is trained in drawing blood and collecting other non-blood specimens for testing.

licensed professional counselor (LPC): LPCs possess a master's or doctoral degree in counseling and will offer collaborative, therapeutic counseling.

licensed clinical social worker (LCSW): LCSWs are licensed to practice in a clinical or counseling setting and directly intermingle with clients to diagnose and treat mental, emotional, and behavioral issues.

occupational therapist registered (OTR): An OTR assists patients as they learn and practice skills for daily living. **physical therapist (PT)**: The PT assists patients with movement.

Quick Review Question

6. A phlebotomist is a medical professional who is trained to perform which of the following tasks?
    A) provide hospice care
    B) draw blood
    C) administer medications
    D) perform moderate- and high-complexity laboratory testing

ANSWER KEY

1. D) is correct. When questioning a patient through an interpreter, whether the patient cannot hear or does not speak English, the nurse aide should always direct questions to the patient.

2. B) is correct. Patients have a right to safe and respectful care, meaning complaints about health care personnel should be addressed promptly. However, the Patient's Bill of Rights does not include the right for patients to choose their nurse.

3. A) is correct. The nurse aide has an ethical duty to report the stolen money to their supervisor but should not directly involve themselves in the situation by talking to the patient or visitor.

4. B) is correct. When a patient opens their mouth to allow their temperature to be taken, they are giving implied consent.

5. A) is correct. Obtaining a stool sample from the patient is within the scope of practice of a nurse aide. The other tasks must be performed by a nurse or physician.

6. B) is correct. A phlebotomist is a medical professional trained to draw blood.

Practice Test #1

1. What is the significance of taring an electric scale when measuring a client's weight?
    a. It powers on the scale prior to use.
    b. It allows the CNA to choose the unit of measurement.
    c. It ensures the scale is at zero before the client's weight is measured.
    d. It rounds the client's weight to the nearest tenth.

2. A patient expresses their wish to discontinue a prescribed medication due to concerns about potential side effects. How should the CNA address the patient's rights?
    a. Advise the patient to follow the healthcare provider's instructions without questioning them.
    b. Encourage the patient to consult with the healthcare provider to discuss their concerns.
    c. Discourage the patient from discontinuing the medication and explain the potential consequences.
    d. Adjust the patient's medication regimen based on their concerns.

3. Which of the following statements made by the CNA would indicate that they may need additional training regarding client ambulation?
    a. "I need to grab the gait belt before we get the client up to the bathroom."
    b. "I assisted the client to the bathroom. I am providing them with privacy and will return when they press the call bell."
    c. "The client uses a walker, so let's make sure we have that in the room first."
    d. "I need to confirm the client's mobility orders with the nurse before we get the client up."

4. While performing a finger stick blood glucose test for a client, the CNA wipes away the first drop of blood from the client's finger. What is the purpose of this step?
    a. It prevents inaccurate results
    b. It prevents client infection
    c. It prevents equipment contamination
    d. It prevents client discomfort

5. The CNA enters a client's room to find that they are unresponsive and not breathing. What is the most appropriate next step the CNA should take?
    a. Check for a pulse
    b. Perform thirty chest compressions
    c. Perform two rescue breaths
    d. Call for help

6. A client has orders for blood glucose monitoring to be performed "AC" and "HS." The abbreviation "AC" indicates that the client has their blood sugar measured when?
    a. At night
    b. In the morning
    c. Before mealtimes
    d. After mealtimes

7. A patient in a healthcare facility has expressed concerns about their privacy and confidentiality. Which of the following actions by the CNA reinforces the patient's rights in this situation?
   a. Limiting the patient's access to their medical records to protect privacy
   b. Sharing the patient's medical information with their family members without consent
   c. Implementing strict security measures to safeguard patient information
   d. Informing the patient about their right to control the disclosure of their health information

8. As the CNA is verifying the client's supplemental oxygen flow rate, they see the measurement is reading 2. What unit of measurement is associated with this client's flow rate?
   a. Milliliter per minute
   b. Milliliter per hour
   c. Liter per minute
   d. Liter per hour

9. The CNA working in the hospital setting overhears a heated argument between two family members of a patient in the CNA's care. The argument is escalating and becoming a disturbance to other patients and staff. What would be the most appropriate course of action?
   a. Join the argument and try to mediate the situation.
   b. Call security immediately to handle the situation.
   c. Attempt to de-escalate the situation and inform the supervising nurse.
   d. Ignore the argument as it is a family matter and not the CNA's responsibility.

10. The CNA has been assigned to care for a female patient who is recovering from a severe car accident and frequently expresses anger and frustration, often lashing out at staff and other patients. She repeatedly states that she blames herself for the accident and the resulting injuries. How should the CNA respond?
    a. Confront the patient about her inappropriate behavior and ask her to control her temper.
    b. Ignore the patient's statements about self-blame, focusing only on her physical care needs.
    c. Reassure the patient that accidents happen, and she shouldn't blame herself.
    d. Provide empathetic care and report her emotional status to the supervising nurse.

11. When washing hands with soap and water, it is important to scrub for a minimum of how many seconds?
    a. Ten seconds
    b. Twenty seconds
    c. Thirty seconds
    d. Forty seconds

12. Which of the following should be AVOIDED when performing perineal hygiene on a female client?
    a. Using a clean portion of the washcloth with each swipe
    b. Choosing a gentle, fragrance-free soap to wash the perineal area
    c. Providing perineal hygiene after each episode of incontinence
    d. Cleansing the vulva starting at the vagina and wiping toward the pubic mound

13. The CNA is caring for a patient with advanced dementia who frequently forgets to eat their meals, leading to weight loss and nutritional deficiencies. As a CNA, which of the following interventions would be MOST appropriate?
    a. Remind the patient at each meal about the importance of nutrition for their health, hoping the information will motivate them to eat.
    b. Provide the patient with frequent meals throughout the day, and encourage them to eat whenever they are awake and somewhat alert.
    c. Insist that the patient must eat their meals at the designated mealtimes, even if they refuse or don't show interest in eating.
    d. Reduce the number of meals per day to avoid overwhelming the patient with too many mealtimes.

14. The CNA obtains vital signs from an elderly client. Which of the following takes PRIORITY in reporting to the nurse?
    a. Oral temperature of 97.3 degrees Fahrenheit
    b. Pulse of 50 bpm
    c. Blood pressure of $\frac{132}{86}$
    d. Respirations of 12 breaths/minute

15. Caring for a patient diagnosed with _____, would require the CNA to perform hand hygiene with soap and water, NOT alcohol-based hand sanitizer.
    a. C. difficile (C. diff)
    b. Influenza (Flu)
    c. Methicillin-resistant Staphylococcus aureus (MRSA)
    d. Viral gastroenteritis (Stomach flu)

16. The CNA is currently precepting a new CNA. Which statement made by the orientee requires additional follow-up to ensure they understand how to safely transfer a client?
    a. "I am just checking to make sure the wheels of the bed are locked."
    b. "I need to grab the gait belt before we begin."
    c. "I need to move some things out of the way before we get them up."
    d. "I will grab a pair of their socks since they do not have shoes."

17. While ambulating, the client loses balance and begins to fall. Which of the following is the LEAST appropriate action by the CNA?
    a. Attempting to gently lower the client to the floor
    b. Attempting to protect the client from hitting their head
    c. Attempting to catch the client to prevent them from falling
    d. Attempting to call for assistance

18. The CNA is preparing to obtain a client's blood pressure. What position should the client's arm be in for the most accurate results?
    a. Above the level of the client's heart
    b. At the level of the client's heart
    c. Below the level of the client's heart
    d. At the client's side

19. The CNA is helping a client walk with a wheeled walker. The client has right-sided weakness. The CNA knows that the client should begin each step by doing what?
   a. Sliding the walker forward
   b. Picking the walker up
   c. Stepping with the weaker leg
   d. Stepping with the stronger leg

20. While assisting a client with washing their face, which technique should the CNA begin with?
   a. Avoid the eye area so the client does not get soap in their eyes.
   b. Use an open washcloth to wipe the face from the forehead to the chin.
   c. Use warm water on a washcloth and begin with the inner eye area.
   d. Exfoliate the skin by scrubbing in circular motions.

21. For which of the following clients would logrolling be most appropriate?
   a. A client who is recovering from a spinal injury
   b. A client who is recovering from a hip replacement
   c. A client who is recovering from abdominal surgery
   d. A client who is recovering from a stroke

22. The CNA observes the primary nurse taking a portion of a patient's prescribed pain medication and discreetly placing it in their pocket. Concerned by their actions, the CNA approaches the nurse and inquires about the reason behind their behavior. The nurse admits to taking the medication for their personal use, claiming they are experiencing occasional pain and lack health insurance to afford their own pain relievers. After speaking with the nurse, the CNA decides to ignore this information and not report it to their supervisor. Given this scenario, which action by the primary nurse would be considered a direct ethical violation?
   a. Taking the patient's prescribed pain medication for personal use
   b. Admitting to unauthorized use of medication to a colleague
   c. Prioritizing personal needs over patient care and safety
   d. Failure to report this information to the supervisor

23. A patient recently received a terminal cancer diagnosis and is experiencing severe emotional distress, alternating between silent despair and tearful breakdowns. What would be the most appropriate response to provide emotional support to the patient?
   a. Attempt to reassure the patient that everything will be okay and that miraculous recoveries happen every day.
   b. Encourage the patient to be strong and accept the situation, reminding them that everyone has to pass at some point.
   c. Sit with the patient, listen empathetically, and acknowledge the patient's feelings without judgment.
   d. Divert the conversation toward a lighter topic each time the patient starts discussing their diagnosis, and attempt to lift their mood.

24. The CNA is assisting a client when they suddenly slump down in bed and do not appear to be breathing. The CNA yells for help and begins to check for the client's pulse at which location?
   a. The wrist
   b. The elbow
   c. The hip
   d. The neck

25. What does a systolic blood pressure measurement represent?
    a. The top number of the blood pressure measurement
    b. The bottom number of the blood pressure measurement
    c. Both the top and bottom number of the blood pressure measurement
    d. The difference between the top and bottom measurement

26. Communication is vital in the healthcare team to ensure the provision of safe and quality care. As a CNA, what is the most appropriate way to communicate with other healthcare team members regarding a patient's condition?
    a. Use complex medical jargon and terminology to ensure accuracy in communication.
    b. Avoid sharing information unless explicitly requested by another team member.
    c. Use clear and concise language to convey patient-related information effectively.
    d. Share patient information with anyone in the healthcare setting to promote collaboration.

27. The CNA is caring for a patient who is cognitively impaired and has difficulty understanding explanations about care procedures. What would be the BEST approach to communicate with this patient?
    a. Use detailed explanations and complex medical terms to ensure clarity.
    b. Speak in a louder voice so the patient can hear better.
    c. Use simple language, demonstrate the procedures, and verify understanding.
    d. Minimize communication with the patient to avoid confusion.

28. In a healthcare team, conflicts may arise due to differences in opinions and perspectives. How should the CNA approach conflicts with other team members?
    a. Avoid addressing conflicts and focus solely on providing patient care.
    b. Confront team members directly and assertively to resolve conflicts immediately.
    c. Seek guidance from a supervisor or team leader to mediate conflicts.
    d. Share the conflicts with other CNAs to gather their opinions and perspectives.

29. Which of the following positions is typically most appropriate for feeding?
    a. Supine
    b. High Fowler's
    c. Dorsal Recumbent
    d. Prone

30. A client's weight is measured as 65 kilograms. What is the client's weight in pounds?
    a. 29.5 lb
    b. 32.5 lb
    c. 130 lb
    d. 143 lb

31. Patient rounding is completed daily by the healthcare team to discuss the progress and needs of each patient. In the context of patient rounding, which of the following professionals is NOT typically involved in these meetings?
    a. Physicians
    b. Nurses
    c. Physical therapists
    d. CNAs

32. What is the PRIMARY reason healthcare workers are advised not to wear artificial nails in the healthcare setting?
    a. It does not appear professional
    b. It can lead to injury to the caregiver
    c. It can lead to safety concerns for clients
    d. It is against policy

33. What is the name of the device used to measure a client's blood oxygen saturation that is often used when obtaining vital signs?
    a. Sphygmomanometer
    b. Pulse oximeter
    c. Stethoscope
    d. Oxygen cannula

34. A client's height is measured as 5 feet and 6 inches. How many inches tall is this client?
    a. 56 in
    b. 65 in
    c. 66 in
    d. 78 in

35. A patient with chronic, severe back pain has started isolating themselves in their room and refusing to participate in any social activities. Considering the CNA understands the importance of social interaction for mental health, how should they approach this situation?
    a. Encourage the patient to participate in group activities, explaining that it's good for them to stay distracted.
    b. Respect the patient's decision to isolate, leave them alone, and report their isolation as a voluntary choice.
    c. Inform the patient that isolation can lead to depressive symptoms and exacerbate their overall condition.
    d. Report the patient's self-isolation to the nurse, expressing concern about the potential negative effects on the patient's mental health.

36. A nurse working on a busy hospital unit approaches the CNA and asks them to administer medication to several patients to distribute the workload. The CNA has received clear instructions by the nurse for medication administration and the nurse ensures the CNA that it is okay even if it is against hospital policy. What should the CNA do in this situation?
    a. Refuse to administer the medication, as it is beyond the CNA's scope of practice.
    b. Accept the task and administer the medication, ensuring it aligns with assigned duties.
    c. Communicate workload concerns to the nurse and ask for guidance on prioritizing tasks.
    d. Decline the task and leave it for another CNA to handle.

37. A client's mobility orders state that the client is "1 assist with walker." The CNA would prepare to assist the client to transfer to the bathroom by:
    a. Grasping the gait belt while the client uses the walker to ambulate to the bathroom.
    b. Asking one additional colleague to accompany the CNA and assist the client with ambulation to the bathroom with their walker.
    c. Observing the client as they use their walker to ambulate to the bathroom.
    d. Supporting the client under the arm as they use their walker to ambulate to the bathroom.

38. A client needs assistance sitting up at the edge of their bed. The CNA turns the client to their side before helping them pivot into a seated position. This maneuver is performed by supporting the client's knees and which other area?
   a. Upper arm
   b. Hands
   c. Shoulders
   d. Neck

39. The CNA is caring for a patient that is observing Ramadan, a month of fasting from dawn to sunset. How should the CNA appropriately handle meal services for this patient?
   a. Serve meals at the usual time and provide the patient with options for breaking their fast after sunset.
   b. Coordinate with the dietary department to accommodate the patient's fasting schedule.
   c. Inform the patient that fasting is not recommended during their hospital stay and encourage them to follow their regular meal routine.
   d. Consult with the patient's religious representative to determine the best approach for meal services during Ramadan.

40. After reviewing a client's diet and activity orders, which of the following is the next step the CNA should take to assist the client with feeding?
   a. Apply a hair net
   b. Apply gloves
   c. Sit at the client's eye level
   d. Wash hands

41. The CNA notices a significant change in the skin integrity of a patient who is at risk for pressure ulcers. What would be an effective way to communicate these findings to the nurse?
   a. Leave a note on the nurse's desk describing the changes.
   b. Contact the primary nurse through a phone call or secure messaging system.
   c. Inform a coworker about the findings and ask them to relay the information to the nurse.
   d. Wait for the primary nurse to return and discuss the findings in person.

42. A patient has been showing signs of mental distress over the last few weeks. The observed signs and symptoms include prolonged sadness, loss of interest in previously enjoyed activities, irregular eating and sleeping patterns, and verbalizing feelings of worthlessness. Based on these observations, what diagnosis would the CNA expect to be discussed among the medical team?
   a. Anxiety disorder
   b. Bipolar disorder
   c. Major depressive disorder
   d. Adjustment disorder

43. A client's oxygen saturation is measuring low, but the client does not appear to be in distress. Which of the following would be LEAST likely to cause false low oxygen saturation measurement?
   a. The client's hands are sweating
   b. The client has dark skin
   c. The client is cold
   d. The client is wearing nail polish

44. Which of the following should the CNA report to the nurse?
    a. A client is napping before dinner.
    b. A client requests a snack before bed.
    c. A client coughs each time they take a bite of food.
    d. A client asks for a different choice for dinner.

45. When performing a manual blood pressure measurement, what is the part that goes around the client's extremity called?
    a. Sphygmomanometer
    b. Cuff
    c. Stethoscope
    d. Bulb

46. A client's pulse is equal to the number of heartbeats per what measurement of time?
    a. Six seconds
    b. Ten seconds
    c. Thirty seconds
    d. Sixty seconds

47. A patient's family member comes to the CNA and demands immediate updates about the patient's health status. How should the CNA handle this situation?
    a. Look at the patient's medical record and share all information available.
    b. Tell them that it is not a top priority and someone will speak with them when they are available.
    c. Inform them that it's against policy to provide medical updates and direct them to the appropriate person.
    d. Ignore the family member's demand and report the situation to the patient.

48. The CNA is caring for a transgender patient that has expressed discomfort with being addressed by their legal name and gender marker. As a CNA, what would be the most appropriate response?
    a. Continue to use the legal name and gender marker in all official documentation, but use their preferred name and pronouns in conversation.
    b. Tell the patient that it is a requirement to use their legal name and gender marker in all circumstances.
    c. Change all the patient's official records to reflect their preferred name and gender pronouns.
    d. Ignore the patient's preferences, as it doesn't affect their medical care.

49. A client with urge incontinence is able to stand and walk for short distances with minimal assistance. Which of the following toileting orders would the CNA anticipate for this client?
    a. Transfer to the bathroom with assistance, following a consistent schedule
    b. Transfer to the bedside commode
    c. Use of bedpan, on a consistent schedule
    d. Use of absorbent pads or underwear

50. After dinner, the CNA enters the room of a client who has orders for blood glucose monitoring before meals. The CNA notices the client's tray remains untouched, and the client appears to be sleeping in their recliner. Attempts to wake the client are unsuccessful. What should the CNA do?
    a. Begin assisting the client with feeding
    b. Attempt to transfer the client back to bed
    c. Call for help
    d. Obtain another blood glucose level

51. Which part of the fingertip is the best location for performing a finger stick for blood glucose monitoring?
    a. The side of the fingertip
    b. The center of the pad of the fingertip
    c. The tip of the finger
    d. The outer edge of the pad of the fingertip

52. During a break, the CNA overhears two nurses discussing a patient's medical condition in a public area where others can hear. What should the CNA do in this situation?
    a. Join the conversation and provide insight into the patient's condition.
    b. Report the incident to the supervisor or the hospital's privacy officer.
    c. Share the information with colleagues to improve teamwork.
    d. Ignore the conversation as it does not directly involve the CNA.

53. The CNA notices that a patient's request for pain medication has been consistently overlooked by the nursing staff. What is the appropriate chain of command for reporting this issue and advocating for the patient's needs?
    a. Inform the charge nurse or nursing supervisor about the situation.
    b. Report the issue to the physician in charge of the patient's care.
    c. Bring the concerns to the attention of the hospital's ethics committee.
    d. Report the issue to the Chief Nursing Officer (CNO) or Director of Nursing.

54. A patient expresses their concerns about feeling disrespected and belittled by a healthcare provider. The patient shares that they were interrupted frequently, their questions were dismissed, and they felt unheard throughout the interaction. Which of the following patient rights is being violated in this situation?
    a. Right to autonomy and self-determination in healthcare decisions
    b. Right to accurate and complete information about their medical condition
    c. Right to a fair and impartial review of any grievances or complaints
    d. Right to participate in research studies and clinical trials if desired

55. Which of the following is NOT an appropriate reason for a caregiver to encourage a client to perform tasks to the best of their ability?
    a. Client dignity
    b. Promotion of autonomy
    c. Provider time management
    d. Preservation and recovery

56. Social outings and art projects are two examples of activities that primarily benefit elderly clients in what way?
    a. They allow healthcare providers to keep an eye on the clients.
    b. They provide opportunities for clients to exercise.
    c. They keep clients from being bored.
    d. They provide a sense of purpose for clients.

57. A patient with a terminal illness has expressed a desire to receive last rites from a priest. However, due to infection control measures, outside visitors are currently restricted at the facility. What is the most appropriate course of action to take as a CNA?
    a. Tell the patient that it's unfortunately not possible due to the current restrictions.
    b. Suggest that a virtual meeting could be arranged with a priest.
    c. Inform the patient that any hospital employee can perform the ritual, as most of them have seen it done before.
    d. Ignore the request, since the CNA is unable to revise the visitor policy.

58. The CNA is assisting a client with feeding. After two bites of their meal, the client states that they are no longer hungry. Which of the following responses would be most appropriate?
    a. "I am sure you are not finished already. Here is another bite of food. You need to eat."
    b. "That is no problem. I will take your tray and get you cleaned up."
    c. "Is there something else you might like better? I see you have a cookie and applesauce on your tray."
    d. "I am going to need to notify the nurse if you are unable to eat more."

59. A patient diagnosed with late-stage Alzheimer's disease frequently exhibits restlessness, irritability, and bouts of yelling, especially in the late afternoon and evening hours. The symptoms seem to worsen during this time. Which of the following terms best describes this phenomenon?
    a. Sundowning
    b. Disruptive behavior
    c. Cognitive decline
    d. Anxiety disorder

60. Which of the following should be IMMEDIATELY reported to the nurse?
    a. Blood sugar measurement of 70 mg/dL
    b. Blood pressure of $\frac{118}{70}$
    c. Weight gain of 5 lb since yesterday
    d. Respirations of 18 breaths/minute

Answer Explanations #1

1. C: Choice C is the correct answer, as taring a scale is to set the scale to zero - removing any unwanted weight (i.e., blanket) - prior to measuring the client's weight. This promotes a more accurate measurement. Choice A is incorrect because taring a scale is not the same as powering on an electric scale. Choice B is incorrect because taring the scale does not have any impact on the unit of measurement used for a client's weight. Lastly, Choice D is not correct because taring a scale does not impact how the measurement is rounded.

2. B: Choice B is the correct answer, as the CNA should respect the patient's autonomy and encourage open communication between the patient and the healthcare provider. Choice A disregards the patient's right to make decisions about their own healthcare. Choice C discourages patient involvement and fails to address their concerns. Choice D exceeds the scope of practice for a CNA and is the responsibility of the healthcare provider.

3. B: Choice B is the correct answer, as this statement may indicate a need for additional training. If a client requires assistance to ambulate to the bathroom, it would be unsafe to leave them unattended. Choice A is not the correct answer because a gait belt is always indicated when assisting a client with transfers and ambulation. Choice C is not the correct answer because it would be appropriate to use a walker if ordered and indicated for client mobility. Choice D is not the correct answer because confirming mobility orders before ambulating a client is safe and appropriate care.

4. A: Choice A is the correct answer because a false high measurement can occur if the finger stick site is not allowed to *fully* dry after the area is cleansed with an alcohol prep pad. To avoid inaccurate results, the first drop of blood is wiped with a clean gauze pad before obtaining the sample. Choices B, C, and D are incorrect because wiping the first drop of blood does not prevent infection, equipment contamination, or discomfort.

5. D: Choice D is the correct answer, as the most appropriate next step the CNA should immediately take is to shout or call for nearby help. Choices A, B, and C are not the correct answers because the CNA should shout for help *before* proceeding to check for a pulse, begin chest compressions, or provide rescue breaths.

6. C: Choice C is the correct answer, as the medical abbreviation "AC" stands for the Latin word *ante cibum*, which means "before meals." Choice A is incorrect because "at night" would be associated with the abbreviation "PM" ("evening") or "HS" ("hour of sleep"). Choice B is incorrect because "morning" would be associated with the abbreviation "AM." Choice D is incorrect because "after mealtimes" would be associated with the abbreviation "PC," which is derived from the Latin term *post cibum*.

7. D: Choice D is the correct answer, as informing the patient about their right to control the disclosure of their health information acknowledges the patient's concerns and empowers them to make decisions regarding their health information. Choice A is inappropriate and can hinder their involvement in their own care. Choice B violates the patient's privacy by sharing information without their consent. Choice C addresses security but does not directly address the patient's concerns about privacy and confidentiality.

8. C: Choice C is the correct answer because supplemental oxygen is measured in liters per minute (L/min). This client is receiving 2 L/min of supplemental oxygen.

9. C: Choice *C* is the correct answer, as the CNA role involves maintaining a peaceful and safe environment for all patients. Attempting to de-escalate the situation and notifying the supervising nurse of the incident are the most appropriate actions. Choice *A* may exacerbate the situation, Choice *B* might escalate the situation unnecessarily, and Choice *D* fails to address a potential safety issue.

10. D: Choice *D* is the correct answer, as it's important to acknowledge and validate the feelings of patients, even if they are challenging. The CNA can provide empathetic care and ensure that the healthcare team is aware of the patient's emotional state. Choice *A* might escalate the situation and doesn't demonstrate understanding or empathy. Choice *B* neglects the importance of addressing mental health needs in conjunction with physical care. Choice *C*, while well-intentioned, could dismiss her feelings instead of helping her process them.

11. B: Choice *B* is the correct answer, as hand hygiene performed with soap and water should be scrubbed for at least twenty seconds. Choice *A* is incorrect because hands should be washed for at least twenty seconds. Choices *C* and *D* are not correct because it is not generally necessary to wash hands for more than twenty seconds unless hands are exceptionally soiled.

12. D: Choice *D* is the correct answer, as the CNA would *avoid* cleansing the vulva by starting at the vagina and wiping up toward the pubic mound. This technique would increase the risk of urinary tract infections. Choices *A*, *B*, and *C* are not the correct answers because it is recommended to use a gentle, fragrance-free soap to cleanse the perineal area, a clean portion of the washcloth should be used with each swipe, and perineal care should be provided after each episode of incontinence.

13. B: Choice *B* is the correct answer, as offering frequent, small, nutrient-dense meals can help ensure that the patient maintains a balanced diet despite their forgetfulness. This approach respects the patient's current cognitive state and strives to meet their nutritional needs effectively. Choices *A*, *C*, and *D* are not ideal because they either overlook the patient's cognitive status or do not adequately address the patient's nutritional needs.

14. B: Choice *B* is the correct answer, as a pulse reading of 50 bpm is significantly below the normal range of approximately 60–100 and would be the highest priority to report to the nurse. Choice *A* is not the correct answer because a temperature of 97.3 degrees Fahrenheit is within normal limits for an elderly client. A blood pressure reading of $\frac{132}{86}$ is considered borderline hypertensive for the client's age but would not be the highest priority to report to the nurse. Respirations of 12 breaths/minute are within the normal range and would not require priority reporting to the nurse.

15. A: Choice *A* is the correct answer, as hand hygiene with soap and water should be always performed when caring for a client with *C. difficile*. The organism responsible for *C. difficile* is a spore that is not inactivated by alcohol-based cleansers. Choices *B*, *C*, and *D* are not correct because these organisms are examples of viruses that can be effectively neutralized by alcohol-based cleansers as well as soap and water.

16. D: Choice *D* is the correct answer, as the new CNA planning to use regular socks for patient ambulation will require additional follow-up for understanding. Regular socks increase the chances of the patient falling, while socks with grips are an appropriate and safe choice when transferring a client. Choices *A*, *B*, and *C* indicate that the orientee understands the principles of safe transfer and does not require additional follow-up by the preceptor.

17. C: Choice *C* is the correct answer, as attempting to catch the client or prevent a fall can result in injury to the client and/or CNA and is the LEAST appropriate action. Choices *A*, *B*, and *D* are appropriate steps to take in the event of a fall, as the CNA can attempt to gently guide the client to the floor while seeking to

support the client's head and body to prevent injury, if possible. The CNA should call for assistance while remaining with the client and not moving them further.

18. B: Choice B is the correct answer, as the extremity being used for obtaining a client's blood pressure should be positioned at the level of the heart for the most accurate result. Choice A is incorrect because placing the extremity above the level of the heart can result in a falsely low blood pressure measurement. Choices C and D are also incorrect because placing the extremity below the level of the heart or at the client's side can result in a false high blood pressure reading.

19. A: Choice A is the correct answer, as each step begins with the walker sliding forward. Choice B is incorrect because the wheeled walker would not be picked up. Choice C is incorrect because the client steps forward with the weaker leg after the walker slides forward. Choice D is incorrect, as the client steps forward with the strong leg only after sliding the walker forward and stepping with the weaker leg first.

20. C: Choice C is the correct answer, as using comfortably warm water on a clean washcloth and starting at the client's inner eye while gently wiping toward the outer eye is the appropriate action. Choice A would be incorrect because it would not be appropriate to avoid washing the eye area. Choice B is incorrect because it is best to begin with a clean washcloth to the eye area before moving to the rest of the face. Choice D would be incorrect because scrubbing and exfoliating the skin should be avoided since it can cause injury or discomfort to the client.

21. A: Choice A is the correct answer, as logrolling is a technique for minimizing movement of the spine while rolling a client. Therefore, a client with a spinal injury would be the most appropriate candidate for logrolling. Choices B, C, and D are incorrect because logrolling is not necessarily indicated for clients with a hip replacement, abdominal surgery, or stroke history.

22. A: Choice A is the correct answer, as the primary nurse's action of taking the patient's prescribed pain medication for personal use directly violates ethical principles and professional standards. While Choice B may be unprofessional and inappropriate, it does not directly constitute an ethical violation. Choice C is ethically problematic, but it is also not the direct violation in this scenario. Choice D is an ethical violation by the CNA, not by the primary nurse.

23. C: Choice C is the correct answer, as healthcare providers should offer empathetic support to patients who are dealing with distressing diagnoses. In this scenario, listening empathetically and acknowledging the patient's feelings without judgment can be a helpful approach. Choices A and B can appear insensitive and dismissive of the patient's feelings, while Choice D may avoid addressing the patient's immediate emotional needs.

24. D: Choice D is the correct answer, as the correct site for checking a client's pulse during an emergency is the neck (the carotid site). It is important to remember that this site should only be palpated for 5-10 seconds, but NO LONGER than 10 seconds. Choice A is incorrect because this is the radial site. This is a commonly used location for standard pulse measurement. Choice B is incorrect because this is the brachial site and is a less common location for assessing pulse in adults. Choice C is incorrect because this is the femoral site which is also a less common location for assessing pulse.

25. A: Choice A is the correct answer, as the systolic blood pressure represents the top number of the blood pressure measurement. For example, if the measurement is $\frac{155}{90}$, the systolic blood pressure would be 155. Choice B is incorrect because the bottom number of the blood pressure measurement is the diastolic blood pressure. Choice C is incorrect because both the bottom and top numbers make up a client's blood pressure measurement. Lastly, Choice D is incorrect because the difference between the top and bottom measurement is called the pulse pressure, which is a reading used by nurses and healthcare providers to identify clients at risk for certain health conditions.

26. C: Choice C is the correct answer, as clear and concise communication is essential to ensure accurate and efficient information exchange within the healthcare team. Choice A may hinder understanding among team members who are not familiar with the terms. Choice B can impede teamwork and compromise patient care. Choice D violates patient confidentiality and privacy.

27. C: Choice C is the correct answer, as the most effective approach is to use simple language, demonstrate the procedures, and verify understanding. This helps overcome communication barriers and ensures the patient comprehends the information. Choice A may confuse the patient further, Choice B may not address the cognitive impairment, and Choice D hinders the provision of necessary care.

28. C: Choice C is the correct answer, as seeking guidance from a supervisor or team leader allows for appropriate intervention and conflict resolution. Choice A does not address the underlying issues and may lead to unresolved tension. Choice B can escalate the situation and hinder teamwork. Choice D may not lead to a satisfactory resolution.

29. B: Choice B is the correct answer, as *High Fowler's* position (client sitting straight up) is typically the safest position for a client to be in during feeding. Choice A is not correct because a *supine* position (lying face-up) while feeding increases the chances of aspiration (taking food into the airway and lungs) or choking. Choice C is not correct because *dorsal recumbent* position (lying down with knees bent) also significantly increases the risk of aspiration and choking. Choice D is incorrect because the *prone* position (lying face-down) would not be safe or appropriate for feeding.

30. D: Choice D is the correct answer, as one kilogram is equal to 2.2 pounds. The CNA calculates the client's weight in pounds by multiplying the weight in kilograms by 2.2, equaling 143 lb. Choices A, B, and C are incorrect.

31. D: Choice D is the correct answer, as CNAs, while essential members of the healthcare team, are typically not directly involved in patient rounding. Their primary responsibilities include assisting with activities of daily living (ADLs), such as bathing, dressing, feeding, and assisting with mobility. While CNAs may provide updates to the nurse related to ADLs or observations during direct care, they are not usually involved in the rounding process. Choices A, B, and C are all integral members during patient rounding.

32. C: Choice C is the correct answer, as the primary reason artificial nails should be avoided in the healthcare setting is that artificial nails pose a safety risk to clients. Long nails, in general, can lead to injuries. Additionally, artificial nails have been shown to harbor bacteria and viruses, even after appropriate hand hygiene has been performed. Choices A, B, and D are not the correct answers as these are examples of secondary reasons artificial nails may not be permitted in healthcare settings.

33. B: Choice B is the correct answer, as a pulse oximeter is a device (often placed on a finger or toe) used to measure a client's blood oxygen saturation level. Choice A is incorrect because a sphygmomanometer is a device used to measure a client's blood pressure. Choice C is incorrect because a stethoscope is a device used to auscultate (listen) for sounds made within the body. Choice D is incorrect because an oxygen cannula is the medical tubing used to deliver supplemental oxygen to a client's nose.

34. C: Choice C is the correct answer, as there are 12 inches in a foot. The CNA calculates the client's height in inches by multiplying 5 feet by 12, which is 60. The remaining 6 inches are added to make a total of 66 inches. Choices A, B, and D are incorrect.

35. D: Choice D is the correct answer. Given the potential negative impact of social isolation on mental health, it's important for the CNA to report such changes in patient behavior to the nurse. This can ensure that the patient's needs are adequately addressed and that necessary interventions are put in place.

Choices A, B, and C may either be ineffective, dismiss the seriousness of the situation, or could potentially exacerbate the patient's emotional state.

36. A: Choice A is the correct answer, as the CNA should work within their defined role and only perform tasks that fall within their training and authorized responsibilities. Administering medication is typically outside the scope of practice for CNAs and should be performed by licensed healthcare professionals such as nurses. Choice B may lead to legal and ethical issues. Choice C is appropriate to ensure safe and efficient care, but it does not address the issue at hand. Choice D is partially correct in that the CNA should decline the task; however, the task should not be delegated to another CNA. In this scenario, the CNA should also report the nurse to the supervisor for inappropriate delegation.

37. A: Choice A is the correct answer, as "1 assist with walker" means that one caregiver should actively assist the client to ambulate with their walker. Choice B is not correct because asking an additional colleague to help would be indicated for a client requiring "2 assist." Choice C would not be correct because only observing as a client ambulates would be considered a "standby assist." Choice D would not be appropriate because it is not recommended to assist a client by holding the clothing or supporting the client under the arms. These techniques can result in client injury.

38. C: Choice C is the correct answer, as the CNA should put an arm across the client's shoulders and knees to safely pivot the client into a seated position at the edge of the bed. Choices A, B, and D are incorrect because supporting the client anywhere other than the shoulders could result in injury to the client.

39. B: Choice B is the correct answer. During Ramadan, it is important to honor and respect the religious practices of individuals who are fasting. The CNA should coordinate with the dietary department to adjust mealtimes and provide appropriate meals for the patient according to their fasting schedule. This demonstrates cultural sensitivity and supports the patient in observing their religious customs while in the healthcare facility. Choices A and C do not reflect cultural sensitivity. While Choice D may be helpful in certain situations, it is not typically the CNA's role to involve religious representatives in determining meal services.

40. D: Choice D is the correct answer, as washing hands is the most appropriate *next* step the CNA should take after reviewing a client's orders. Choice A is not correct because it is not universally required for the CNA to apply a hair net to assist with feeding. Choice B is not correct because the CNA must wash their hands before applying gloves and after removing gloves. Choice C is not correct because the CNA would need to wash their hands before sitting down at a client's eye level for feeding.

41. B: Choice B is the correct answer, as contacting the primary nurse through a phone call or secure messaging system would be an effective way to communicate these findings as a CNA regarding the significant change in the patient's skin integrity. It allows for direct and immediate communication with the nurse, ensuring that the information is relayed promptly and accurately. Choice A may result in a delay of communication, as the nurse may not immediately see the note. Choice C introduces an extra layer of communication that can lead to potential miscommunication or delays in conveying the critical information to the nurse. Choice D may also result in a significant delay in addressing the issue, especially if the nurse is unavailable for an extended period.

42. C: Choice C is the correct answer, as the patient's prolonged sadness, loss of interest in previously enjoyed activities, irregular eating and sleeping patterns, and verbalization of feelings of worthlessness align with some of the primary diagnostic criteria for major depressive disorder. The CNA should be in communication with the medical team to ensure all disciplines are aware of the patient's symptoms so that appropriate diagnostics and treatments can be initiated. Choices A, B, and D are incorrect because they are not consistent with the patient's observed signs and symptoms.

43. A: Choice A is the correct answer, as sweating is the least likely cause for false low oxygen saturation measurement. Choices B, C, and D are not correct because these are examples of factors that can cause false low oxygen saturation measurements.

44. C: Choice C is the correct answer, as the CNA should report a client who coughs when eating and/or drinking. This could indicate that the client is having trouble swallowing, and this needs to be assessed by the nurse. Choices A, B, and D do not require the CNA to notify the nurse and are not the correct choice.

45. B: Choice B is the correct answer, as the portion of the device that goes around the client's extremity for measuring blood pressure manually is called the cuff. Choice A is incorrect because a *sphygmomanometer* is the entire apparatus used to measure blood pressure manually. Choice C is incorrect because a *stethoscope* is an instrument used to listen for the sounds associated with the blood pressure measurement when using the sphygmomanometer. Choice D is incorrect because the *bulb* is the part of the device that is squeezed to inflate the cuff when preparing to measure the client's blood pressure.

46. D: Choice D is the correct answer, as the pulse is equal to the number of heartbeats in one minute *(sixty seconds)*. The total pulse rate is not equal to the number of heartbeats in six, ten, or thirty seconds; therefore, Choices A, B, and C are incorrect.

47. C: Choice C is the correct answer, as the correct response is to politely inform the family member that it's against policy for the CNA to provide medical updates and direct them to the appropriate person. Choice A may violate patient privacy and would also be better handled by the nurse. Choices B and D are dismissive and do not address the situation appropriately.

48. A: Choice A is the correct answer, as it is important to respect a patient's gender identity. While official documentation might require legal names and gender markers, the CNA should respect and use the patient's preferred name and pronouns in all personal conversations. Choices B and D dismiss the patient's rights to be treated with dignity and respect, while Choice C is outside the scope of a CNA's role and could lead to confusion in the patient's medical care.

49. A: Choice A is the correct answer, as transferring to the bathroom with assistance allows the client to operate at their highest level of functioning, while following a consistent schedule helps the client with bladder training (an intervention to help relieve symptoms of certain types of urinary incontinence). Choice B is incorrect as it is less likely that the bedside commode will be indicated for the client if they can stand and walk short distances. The use of a bedpan, Choice C, would be appropriate for someone who is continent but unable to transfer to a bedside commode or walk to the bathroom. Lastly, Choice D would be incorrect because the use of absorbent pads or underwear should not be used in place of toileting orders.

50. C: Choice C is the correct answer, as the CNA should call for help immediately. The tray is untouched, meaning the client has not eaten. If this client has received sliding scale insulin coverage prior to the meal and did not eat, their blood sugar may have dropped dangerously low. This is an emergency and requires immediate assistance. Choice A is incorrect because the client should not be given any oral food or beverage while they are not alert. Choice B is also incorrect because it would be unsafe to transfer the client, and this would also not be a priority intervention. Choice D is incorrect because the CNA should prioritize calling for help immediately, remaining with the client, monitoring for breathing and circulation, and awaiting further orders once help arrives.

51. D: Choice D is the correct answer, as the outer edge of the fleshy portion of the fingertip is the best location for performing a finger stick for blood glucose monitoring due to it being less sensitive and more likely to provide a quality blood sample. The fingertip and center of the pad of the fingertip should be avoided because these areas are more sensitive and can remain sensitive well after the finger stick procedure is performed, making Choices C and B incorrect. The side of the fingertip should be avoided because this area is less vascular and can make obtaining a sample more difficult, making Choice A incorrect.

52. B: Choice B is the correct answer, as overhearing a conversation about a patient's medical condition in a public area violates patient confidentiality, which should be reported. Choice A further contributes to the breach of confidentiality, Choice C is inappropriate because it disregards patient privacy, and Choice D does not address the ethical concern at hand.

53. A: Choice A is the correct answer, as the charge nurse or nursing supervisor is responsible for overseeing the nursing staff and addressing patient care concerns. They have the authority to investigate and take appropriate action to ensure the patient's request for pain medication is addressed promptly. Choices B, C, and D do not follow the appropriate chain of command.

54. A: Choice A is the correct answer, as the patient's concerns about feeling disrespected, belittled, and unheard by the healthcare provider highlight a violation of their right to autonomy and self-determination. This right emphasizes that patients have the right to be involved in decisions about their own healthcare, including being fully informed, having their questions answered, and having their preferences and values respected. When a healthcare provider dismisses the patient's questions and interrupts them, it undermines their ability to exercise autonomy and participate in their care. Choices B, C, and D do not accurately describe the patient right that is being violated in this scenario.

55. C: Choice C is the correct answer because enhancement of caregiver time management (i.e., freeing up time for the healthcare provider to care for other clients) is NOT a primary reason for encouraging clients to perform care tasks to their level of ability. Choices A and B are not the correct answers because encouraging clients to perform self-care tasks at their level of ability does promote dignity and autonomy. Choice D is not the correct answer either, as encouraging clients to perform care appropriately does preserve the client's ability and it can also aid in the client's recovery.

56. D: Choice D is the correct answer, as social outings and art projects primarily benefit elderly clients by creating a sense of purpose and fulfillment. Choices A, B, and C are incorrect because these are not primary benefits to clients.

57. B: Choice B is the correct answer, as in a situation where a patient wishes to engage in a religious ritual that requires an external visitor, leveraging technology to facilitate a virtual meeting is the best course of action. This approach respects the patient's spiritual needs while adhering to infection control measures. Choices A and D are incorrect, as they disregard the patient's spiritual needs. Choice C oversteps the CNA's role and may not properly fulfill the religious requirements of the last rites.

58. C: Choice C is the correct answer, as it is the *most* appropriate response to make because it encourages the client to eat more, while not forcing the client to eat. It also provides suggestions to encourage additional intake. Choice A is not appropriate because a client should not be forced to eat if they refuse. Choice B is not the most appropriate response because clients should be encouraged to complete their meals. Choice D is not the most appropriate response because coercing and threatening are not appropriate actions for encouraging food intake.

59. A: Choice A is the correct answer, as sundowning refers to a common pattern seen in individuals with Alzheimer's disease, in which they experience increased agitation, restlessness, irritability, and behavioral disturbances during the late afternoon and evening hours. The symptoms tend to worsen or become more pronounced during this time period, especially outside of a schedule or routine environment. Choices B, C, and D do not accurately describe the phenomenon that this patient is experiencing.

60. C: Choice *C* is the correct answer, as significant weight changes require immediate reporting to the nurse. Choices *A* and *B* are not the correct answer because these measurements are within normal limits. Choice *D* is slightly above normal limits but would not require immediate reporting to the nurse unless the client is in distress.

Practice Test #2

1. While assisting a healthcare provider in administering medication to a patient, the CNA notices a significant documentation error that results in an incorrect dosage being administered. The patient is recovering from surgery and heavily relies on accurate medication administration. However, the CNA has reservations about reporting the error due to concerns about potential legal implications. What legal obligations exist for a CNA regarding reporting medication errors in this scenario?
    a. The CNA is legally required to report any observed medication errors promptly, regardless of potential legal implications.
    b. The CNA has the option to choose whether to report the medication error based on their personal judgment.
    c. The CNA is not legally obligated to report the medication error unless it directly causes harm to the patient.
    d. The CNA should report the medication error only if it is likely to result in legal action against the healthcare provider.

2. The CNA preceptor would intervene after observing which of the following during the use of client lift equipment?
    a. The orientee supports the client's weight with their arms while the client is being lowered.
    b. The orientee opens the base legs of the lift equipment prior to transferring the client.
    c. The orientee selects a slightly smaller sling because the client is in between sizes.
    d. The orientee lifts the client a few inches off the bed and checks positioning and client comfort.

3. The CNA is removing a pair of soiled gloves after providing incontinence care for a client. What is the appropriate technique for removing the SECOND soiled glove?
    a. Pinch the cuff near the wrist using the fingers of the clean hand.
    b. Use a clean paper towel to grasp the dirty glove and pull it off.
    c. Use the fingers of the clean hand to push under the cuff to remove the dirty glove.
    d. Apply a clean glove to the clean hand before removing the dirty glove.

4. The CNA has assisted a client to the bathroom and is now preparing to assist with perineal care. There are no more cleansing wipes or washcloths in the client's bathroom or room. What should the CNA do next?
    a. Use the call bell to request a colleague bring the supplies.
    b. Retrieve the cleansing wipes and return to provide perineal care.
    c. Assist the client back to bed before retrieving the cleansing wipes.
    d. Assist the client back to bed and stock the bathroom for next time.

5. When preparing to use lift equipment, what is the MINIMUM number of caregivers that should be present?
    a. One
    b. Two
    c. Three
    d. Four

6. The CNA is assisting a physician in the care of a patient. During the process, the physician asks the CNA for their opinion on the patient's condition and possible treatment options. The CNA has a strong understanding of medical terminology and the patient's current condition. What should the CNA do FIRST?
   a. Share opinions without hesitation, as the CNA is frequently involved in patient care.
   b. Tell the physician that their request is beyond the CNA scope of practice.
   c. Ignore the physician's request and continue with assigned tasks.
   d. Direct the physician to consult with the patient first and then discuss in further detail outside of the patient room.

7. A member of the healthcare team gives the CNA an instruction that is beyond the CNA's scope of practice. What should the CNA do in this situation?
   a. Follow the instructions to show a willingness to learn.
   b. Refuse to carry out the task and report the incident to the supervisor.
   c. Ask a fellow CNA to perform the task instead.
   d. Ignore the instruction and continue with routine tasks.

8. Which of the following would the CNA need to prioritize reporting to the nurse?
   a. The CNA assisted a client with a bed bath.
   b. A confused client was asking for his wife.
   c. The CNA notices a client's tailbone area is pink.
   d. Barrier cream was applied to the client's perineal area.

9. The CNA positions the patient in Fowler's position by doing what?
   a. Positioning the client's knees and upper body flat in bed.
   b. Positioning the client on their side with a pillow between their legs.
   c. Positioning the client's upper body flat and knees bent.
   d. Positioning the client's head of the bed up to a semi-seated position.

10. A patient who has been actively participating in group activities for several weeks has recently started refusing to leave their room. They don't seem upset or unwell, but they consistently decline invitations to join activities. What should the CNA's priority be in this scenario?
    a. Encourage the patient to discuss their feelings and any potential issues that might have caused this change in behavior.
    b. Firmly remind the patient about the importance of group activities for their well-being and insist that they participate.
    c. Respect the patient's current wish for solitude and allow them to stay in their room without trying to persuade them otherwise.
    d. Coordinate with the recreational therapist to bring individual activities to the patient's room to encourage them to engage in some form of stimulation.

11. A patient with advanced dementia seems distressed and consistently refuses a particular caregiver's assistance. How should the CNA best approach this situation while considering the patient's well-being and comfort?
    a. Assign a different caregiver to assist the patient to see if their response improves.
    b. Document the patient's refusal and communicate with the interdisciplinary team to explore alternative approaches.
    c. Convince the patient that the caregiver is qualified and trustworthy, encouraging them to accept the assistance.
    d. Advise the caregiver to persistently attempt to provide care, as familiarity can help alleviate the patient's distress.

12. The CNA is assisting with the collection of a clean catch urine sample for a female client. After assisting the client to cleanse the perineum, the CNA uses which of the following techniques to collect a urine specimen?
   a. Collect the sample once the client has voided completely.
   b. Collect the first stream of urine.
   c. Collect the sample midstream after the client just begins to void.
   d. Collect the sample at any time while the client is voiding.

13. A patient has begun to show signs of obsessive-compulsive behavior. They repeatedly wash their hands until they are raw and become anxious when they are unable to do so. This behavior is new and seems to be causing them distress. As a CNA, what would be the best approach in this situation?
   a. Try to distract the patient each time they start washing their hands in an attempt to break the cycle.
   b. Directly confront the patient about their irrational behavior and insist they stop immediately.
   c. Attempt to maintain a calm environment, gently redirect the patient when possible, and report the behavior to the nurse.
   d. Ignore the behavior as long as it isn't causing physical harm to the patient or others; it might be a phase that will pass.

14. The CNA assists the client back to their room after a therapy session. The client is crying and states, "I am just so tired, and I feel like I'm never going to get better!" Which of the following statements by the CNA is most appropriate?
   a. "You will be fine. Keep working hard, and you will get better!"
   b. "You shouldn't feel bad because you are doing great!"
   c. "I can imagine this must feel overwhelming for you. Progress can be slow, but you are doing a great job!"
   d. "I have seen many other clients with worse diagnoses get better, so I know you can do it!"

15. In which of the following situations would the CNA NOT be required to perform hand hygiene?
   a. The CNA just removed gloves after assisting a client to the bathroom.
   b. The CNA entered a client's room to answer their call light.
   c. The CNA is assisting the client with washing their face after assisting them with putting on their socks.
   d. The CNA is speaking with a client who is standing outside of their room.

16. A client is requesting assistance to go to the bathroom. The CNA is busy and she knows that this client requires additional time and assistance. What would be the most appropriate response by the CNA?
   a. Notify a colleague that she will be assisting the client to the bathroom, and it may take additional time.
   b. Assist the client to use a bedpan.
   c. Notify the client that she will come back when able and remind them that the pad underneath can be changed if necessary.
   d. Ask a colleague to help with the client's request.

17. A nurse is heard shouting that she needs help in a client's room. The CNA arrives to find the nurse performing chest compressions. When performing Basic Life Support (BLS), the individual performing chest compressions should be rotated out at least how often?
    a. Every thirty seconds
    b. Every two minutes
    c. Every five minutes
    d. Every ten minutes

18. The CNA is responding to a client's call. The client asks, "Can I have my pain medicine?" Which of the following would be an example of closed-loop communication?
    a. "I can see if your nurse is available if you'd like."
    b. "Yes."
    c. "I am sorry, but I am unable to get your pain medicine."
    d. "I notified the nurse, and she will be in shortly."

19. A patient under the CNA's care is nearing the end of life. Their family has expressed that they want to perform a spiritual ritual that involves singing and chanting in the patient's room. However, there are strict quiet hours in the facility and other patients nearby who might be disturbed. How should the CNA handle this situation?
    a. Allow the family to perform the ritual regardless of the quiet hours policy.
    b. Deny the family's request as it would disturb other patients.
    c. Suggest the family perform the ritual in a more suitable location outside of the facility.
    d. Discuss the situation with the supervisor, expressing the family's request while taking the needs of other patients into consideration.

20. When performing a bed bath for a client, which of the following techniques is used to promote both privacy AND comfort?
    a. Use an appropriate temperature of water.
    b. Warm the room to a comfortable temperature.
    c. Close the door and/or pull the curtain to the room.
    d. Expose and clean one area at a time.

21. The CNA is assisting a blind client. Which of the following interventions is most likely to help increase the client's ability to perform self-care?
    a. Use bright lighting in the room.
    b. Use larger-size fonts on written materials.
    c. Use bright colors to designate important items.
    d. Set the room up in a predictable way.

22. The CNA is documenting a client's intake for lunch. In addition to eating 75% of their meal, the client drank 4 ounces of orange juice, an 8-ounce nutrition shake, and an 8-ounce glass of water. What is the client's total liquid intake in *milliliters (mL)*?
    a. 44 mL
    b. 240 mL
    c. 300 mL
    d. 600 mL

23. A client has a dietary status of "NPO." The CNA knows that this client should follow which of the following dietary orders?
    a. They may not have any food or liquid.
    b. They may only have soft foods and thickened liquids.
    c. They may have liquids only.
    d. They may have any food or liquid.

24. A patient scheduled for a major surgical procedure in two days has been exhibiting signs of fear and anxiety, often talking about potential complications and worst-case scenarios. How can the CNA best provide stress relief in this situation?
    a. Sit with the patient and allow them to openly talk about their concerns
    b. Educate the patient on the detailed steps of the surgical procedure.
    c. Provide information about support groups or counseling services available to patients preparing for surgery to help address their fears and concerns.
    d. Encourage the patient to maintain a healthy routine with regular exercise, nutritious meals, and sufficient sleep to promote overall well-being and reduce stress levels.

25. Which of the following requests made by the diabetic client's family would the CNA need to question?
    a. They are requesting lotion for the client's legs and feet.
    b. They are requesting an extra blanket for the client.
    c. They are requesting a heating pad for the client.
    d. They ask if the client can have another pair of non-skid socks.

26. Which of the following is the best definition for *assistive devices*?
    a. They are tools used by clients to perform activities of daily living.
    b. They are tools used by caregivers to assist clients with care.
    c. They are resources in the healthcare facility to allow for client monitoring.
    d. They are resources added to public environments to increase general accessibility.

27. Which of the following clients would most likely benefit from passive range of motion movements?
    a. A client receiving physical therapy and rehabilitation for a knee replacement
    b. A client with advanced-stage multiple sclerosis who is bedridden
    c. A client who is receiving intravenous antibiotics for a urinary tract infection
    d. A client who is receiving nursing care for treatment of a leg wound

28. What is the primary reason behind turning a client who cannot reposition themselves?
    a. Circulation
    b. Mobility
    c. Breathing
    d. Comfort

29. A therapeutic recreational activity is scheduled as part of the patient's treatment plan. However, the patient refuses to participate, dismissing the activity as "childish" and "pointless." What would be the most appropriate action for the CNA to take in this situation?
   a. Insist that the patient participate in the activity, as it has been included in their treatment plan by the medical professionals in charge of their care.
   b. Agree with the patient's assessment of the activity and suggest that they skip it, so as not to make them feel uncomfortable.
   c. Validate the patient's feelings, explain the therapeutic benefits of the activity, and encourage them to give it a try.
   d. Report the patient's refusal to participate in the therapeutic activity to the nursing supervisor to ensure appropriate adjustments can be made to their care plan.

30. The CNA responds to a "CODE BLUE" announcement in a client's room. The CNA most likely expects to assist with which of the following?
   a. Assisting the client with a request for a drink.
   b. Assisting a client with toileting.
   c. Assisting with cardiopulmonary resuscitation.
   d. Assisting with a combative client.

31. When speaking with a client who has hearing loss, which of the following is MOST appropriate for increasing the client's comprehension?
   a. Speak loudly to the client to ensure they can hear.
   b. Speak to the client from five feet away.
   c. Speak clearly and avoid speaking too quickly.
   d. Reduce the volume of the television.

32. What is the CNA's role in promoting quality improvement within the healthcare team?
   a. Conduct independent research and develop new treatment protocols.
   b. Share feedback and suggestions for improvement based on direct observations and experiences.
   c. Implement changes in policies and procedures without consulting other team members.
   d. Lead quality improvement meetings and ask team members for input on organizational performance.

33. Which of the following is MOST likely to impact the accuracy of an oral temperature reading?
   a. Timing of last food or beverage
   b. The client's age
   c. The temperature of the client's environment
   d. The client's health status

34. The CNA is providing care for a patient with severe anxiety who has a surgery scheduled tomorrow. The patient is extremely worried and having trouble sleeping. As a CNA, what would be the best course of action?
   a. Suggest the patient try counting sheep to fall asleep.
   b. Reassure the patient and provide them with information about the surgery to help alleviate their worries.
   c. Tell the patient to stop worrying because the surgeons are highly skilled.
   d. Inform the supervising nurse of the patient's state.

35. A patient requests a copy of their medical records for personal reference. How should the CNA proceed?
    a. Deny the patient's request, as medical records are the property of the healthcare facility.
    b. Charge a fee for providing the patient with a copy of their medical records.
    c. Provide the patient with the necessary forms and guidelines to request their medical records.
    d. Inform the patient that they do not have the right to access their own medical records due to confidentiality policies.

36. The CNA is asked to assist a client with ambulation. When the CNA enters the room, the client refuses to get up, stating that they are in too much pain. Which of the following is the most appropriate response by the CNA?
    a. "Your doctor has ordered you to get up. You need to walk to get better."
    b. "I can let your nurse know about your pain. I will come back in an hour to see how you are feeling."
    c. "I am going to have to let your nurse know that you have refused."
    d. "I can come back later."

37. A patient requests the assistance of the CNA in completing their will. How should the CNA respond?
    a. Assist the patient to gain their trust.
    b. Ignore the request, as it is beyond the CNA's scope of practice.
    c. Politely explain that it is beyond the CNA's professional boundaries.
    d. Help the patient and then discuss their wishes with their family.

38. The CNA is caring for a patient who practices Buddhism and is in severe pain due to an advanced illness. The patient requests a quiet space for meditation to help manage the pain. How should the CNA respond?
    a. Arrange a quiet, peaceful space where the patient can meditate undisturbed.
    b. Tell the patient that meditation isn't scientifically proven to manage pain.
    c. Suggest other forms of relaxation like watching TV or reading books.
    d. Ignore the patient's request since pain medication will be more effective.

39. The CNA is attending a care team meeting where the care plans of various patients are being discussed. What is the role of the CNA in this meeting?
    a. The CNA should not participate since they are not a registered nurse.
    b. The CNA should share their observations and insights about the patients' conditions and responses to care.
    c. The CNA should propose changes in medical treatment plans for the patients.
    d. The CNA should sit quietly and take notes of the plans discussed by the registered nurses.

40. During shift change reporting, the CNA giving report seems rushed and provides minimal information about the patients. What should the CNA receiving report do in this situation?
    a. Accept the information and figure out the rest during the shift.
    b. Ask the CNA to slow down and provide more detailed information.
    c. Complain to the nurse about the CNA's behavior.
    d. Ignore the handover and read the patients' chart.

41. The CNA is changing a client's linens when the client mentions that they have been considering harming themselves. What is the most appropriate next action for the CNA to take?
    a. Call for help immediately.
    b. Complete the linen change.
    c. Go find and notify the nurse.
    d. Ask the client to explain their statement.

42. A patient wants to express their concerns about their care and the assigned CNA continually dismisses their concerns as irrelevant. Which patient right is being violated in this scenario?
    a. Right to autonomy and self-determination in healthcare decisions
    b. Right to access and obtain copies of their medical records for review
    c. Right to privacy and confidentiality of personal health information
    d. Right to voice grievances and have them addressed

43. A CNA is assisting the nurse with a routine dressing change for a client's heel wound. While removing the dressing, the client remarks that the area does not usually hurt but is now uncomfortable. Additionally, the CNA notices that the area seems redder than it was two days ago. What is the most appropriate next step for the CNA to take?
    a. Replace the client's previous dressing.
    b. Notify the nurse immediately.
    c. Document the observations.
    d. Finish the dressing change procedure.

44. A client is on a clear liquid diet. Which of the following is NOT a clear liquid?
    a. Jell-O
    b. Chicken broth
    c. Yogurt
    d. Popsicles

45. When assisting a client with walking, which of the following is the correct location for placement of a gait belt?
    a. Around the client's hips
    b. Under the client's breasts
    c. At the client's waist
    d. At the client's belly button

46. A patient expresses concerns about feeling excluded from decisions regarding their treatment plan. Which of the following actions performed by the CNA best supports the patient's right to make a treatment choice while considering the principles of informed consent and shared decision-making?
    a. Conduct independent research on treatment options and present the findings to the patient.
    b. Document the patient's concerns and inform the charge nurse or the attending physician.
    c. Act as a mediator between the patient and the healthcare team, facilitating open and honest communication to ensure the patient's voice is heard.
    d. Encourage the patient to seek a second opinion from another healthcare provider to ensure they have all the necessary information to make an informed choice.

47. The CNA is assisting a client with left-sided paralysis with dressing. What is the first step when removing the client's shirt?
    a. Pull the collar of the shirt over the client's head.
    b. Pull the client's left arm through the shirt sleeve.
    c. Pull the client's right arm through the shirt sleeve.
    d. Pull the shirt up over the arms and head at the same time.

48. Maintaining professional boundaries is crucial for providing ethical and effective care. How can the CNA ensure that appropriate professional boundaries with patients are maintained?
    a. Share personal experiences and opinions to build rapport with patients.
    b. Establish clear physical boundaries and avoid any personal touch that may be misinterpreted.
    c. Engage in social interactions and activities with patients outside of the healthcare setting.
    d. Disclose personal contact information to patients to foster a closer relationship.

49. The CNA is assisting a client with putting their nasal cannula back on. The client says, "Can you turn the oxygen tank up to four liters, please?" What is the most appropriate response by the CNA?
    a. Tell the client, "I am sorry, I am not authorized to do that."
    b. Adjust the client's oxygen level.
    c. Tell the client, "You may adjust the level."
    d. Let the client know that the nurse will be notified.

50. The CNA is assisting a patient with a physical disability to eat their meal. The patient becomes frustrated and says some harsh words out of annoyance. Which of the following actions by the CNA best demonstrates active listening?
    a. Offer reassurance and validation by saying, "I understand how frustrating it can be. Don't worry, I'll finish up quickly."
    b. Give the patient space and time to calm down before continuing with the meal assistance.
    c. Respond empathetically by saying, "It seems like you're feeling frustrated. Could you please explain more about what's bothering you?"
    d. Redirect the conversation to a different topic to distract the patient from their frustration.

51. When caring for a client with an indwelling urinary catheter, the CNA knows that the client is at the HIGHEST risk for what?
    a. Infection
    b. Skin breakdown
    c. Dehydration
    d. Hemorrhage

52. The CNA encounters a situation where a patient's family member, who is also a nurse, requests access to the patient's medical records. The family member insists that their professional background justifies the request and assures the CNA that they have the patient's best interests in mind. In this situation, it is crucial to have a clear understanding of HIPAA (Health Insurance Portability and Accountability Act). What does HIPAA encompass, and how should the CNA respond in this situation?
    a. HIPAA is a law that protects the privacy and security of a patient's health information and sets standards for its electronic exchange. In this case, the CNA should respectfully decline the family

member's request, emphasizing the importance of patient privacy and confidentiality under HIPAA regulations.

b. HIPAA is a policy that ensures patients have access to affordable health insurance coverage. In this case, the CNA can grant the family member's request, as it aligns with the goal of HIPAA to facilitate patient access to healthcare services.

c. HIPAA is a regulation that governs the qualifications and licensing requirements for healthcare professionals. In this case, the CNA should comply with the family member's request, as their professional background grants them access to patient records.

d. HIPAA is a guideline that outlines the appropriate communication methods between healthcare providers and patients. In this case, it is acceptable to provide the family member with access to the patient's medical records, adhering to the communication guidelines outlined in HIPAA.

53. The CNA has been instructed by a client's nurse to change a routine dressing to the posterior upper arm. The CNA knows that the posterior part of the arm will be on which side of the arm?
   a. Front
   b. Back
   c. Inside
   d. Outside

54. The CNA is assisting a client with putting their nasal cannula on. After positioning the prongs into the client's nostrils, what does the CNA do next?
   a. Secure the tubing loosely under the client's chin.
   b. Secure the strap around the back of the client's head.
   c. Place the tubing behind the client's ears.
   d. Position the tubing in front of the client's chest.

55. While providing client care, the CNA can MOST effectively prevent the spread of infection by doing which of the following?
   a. Appropriate use of hand hygiene
   b. Appropriate use of gloves
   c. Staying home when ill
   d. Obtaining all appropriate vaccines

56. While assisting a client back to their room following physical therapy, the CNA notices the client seems disoriented, which is new for this client. Which of the following should the CNA prioritize next?
   a. Remind the client where they are.
   b. Notify the nurse.
   c. Offer to call a family member.
   d. Provide the client with a cold drink.

57. Which task is outside the scope of a CNA's responsibilities?
   a. Assisting the patient with daily grooming and hygiene routine.
   b. Checking the patient's blood glucose level using the glucometer.
   c. Interpreting the patient's vital signs, such as temperature and blood pressure.
   d. Assisting the patient with mobility and ambulation.

58. Which of the following has the LOWEST risk of skin breakdown related to immobility?
    a. Back of head
    b. Sacrum
    c. Wrists
    d. Heels

59. The CNA responds to a call light. The client is alert and oriented. Which technique is most appropriate for verifying this client's identity?
    a. Ask the client to recite their name and birthday while writing it down.
    b. Compare the client's medical record to the client's armband to confirm name and birthday.
    c. Read the client's name and birthday aloud and ask the client to confirm.
    d. Visually inspect the client's armband while the client verbalizes their name and birthday.

60. A patient who was diagnosed with a chronic illness six months ago is frequently tearful and expresses feelings of hopelessness and despair, stating that they see no point in continuing treatment. Based on their emotional state, which stage of grief is the patient likely experiencing?
    a. Denial
    b. Anger
    c. Depression
    d. Acceptance

Answer Explanations #2

1. A: Choice A is the correct answer, as the CNA has a legal obligation to report any observed medication errors promptly, regardless of potential legal implications. Reporting medication errors is crucial for patient safety and adherence to legal and regulatory requirements. It is the CNA's professional duty to prioritize patient well-being and promptly address any errors to prevent harm. Choice B is incorrect, as reporting medication errors is not a matter of personal judgment for a CNA. Choice C is incorrect, as there is a legal duty to report observed medication errors promptly regardless of immediate harm. Choice D is incorrect because error reporting should not be contingent upon the likelihood of legal action against the healthcare provider.

2. A: Choice A is the correct answer because supporting the client's weight during the use of the lift equipment can result in strap displacement and client injury. Choice B is not the answer because widening the base legs increases the stability of the equipment. Choice C is not the correct answer because selecting a slightly smaller sling for a client who is in-between sizes is safer than selecting a sling that is too large. Selecting a sling that is too large for the client can cause the client to slip out of the sling, which can result in serious injury and death. Choice D is not the correct answer because it is best practice to lift the client a few inches off the bed and pause to check positioning and client comfort.

3. C: Choice C is the correct answer, as the most appropriate method of removing the second soiled glove is to carefully push the soiled glove off by slipping the fingers of the clean hand under the cuff of the soiled glove. It is important to take care to avoid touching the outside surface of the soiled glove. Choice A is incorrect because pinching any outside surface of a contaminated glove contaminates the clean hand. Choice B is incorrect because a paper towel does not prevent contamination of the clean hand and is a waste of supplies. Choice D is not the best answer because the clean glove would become contaminated by removing the soiled glove and would then contaminate the clean hand upon removal.

4. A: Choice A is the correct answer, as the most appropriate choice would be to use the call system to notify a colleague to assist with retrieving the supplies. Choice B is incorrect because the client should not be left alone in the bathroom. Choice C is incorrect because it would not be best to bring the client back to bed before performing perineal care. Choice D is also not correct because it would not be appropriate to put off perineal care until the next bathroom trip.

5. B: Choice B is the correct answer, as it is advised to have a minimum of two caregivers present while utilizing lift equipment. Choice A is incorrect because there should be at least two caregivers present. Choices C and D are incorrect because it may not be required to have three or four caregivers present during the operation of lift equipment. However, it is important to note that the CNA should use safe judgment and utilize the number of caregivers required to safely operate this equipment.

6. B: Choice B is the correct answer, as providing opinions on medical conditions and treatment options is beyond the scope of practice for a CNA. Choice A and Choice D can compromise patient care and also demonstrates a violation of the CNA's scope of practice. Choice C does not address the underlying issue.

7. B: Choice B is the correct answer, as the correct response is to refuse to carry out the task and report the incident to the supervisor. It is important to work within the defined role and not perform tasks beyond training and qualifications. Choice A can compromise patient safety, Choice C may put the other CNA in a similar situation, and Choice D disregards the need to address the issue.

8. C: Choice C is the priority item to report to the nurse, as an area of discoloration on a bony area (i.e., sacrum, heels, etc.) could be evidence of skin breakdown due to pressure. This needs to be immediately reported and monitored. Communication between caregivers is key to high-quality client care; therefore, all of the answer choices should be communicated. However, Choices A, B, and D would not be the correct answers because they are expected and would not be the priority.

9. D: Choice D describes the Fowler's position, which is a semi-seated position. Choice A is incorrect as this describes a supine position. Choice B is incorrect as this describes a lateral position. Choice C is incorrect because this position describes the dorsal recumbent position.

10. A: Choice A is the correct answer, as encouraging the patient to express their feelings can help identify any potential issues that may have led to this change in behavior. This empathetic and non-judgmental approach promotes open communication and helps in providing personalized care. Choices B, C, and D might either pressure the patient, disregard their emotional state, or fail to address potential underlying issues.

11. B: Choice B is the correct answer. When a patient with advanced dementia consistently refuses a particular caregiver's assistance, it is essential to prioritize the patient's well-being and comfort. Documenting the patient's refusal helps maintain accurate records and provides valuable information for the interdisciplinary team to assess the situation and develop alternative strategies. Choice A is a valid consideration, but it fails to address the underlying causes of the patient's distress. Choice C does not respect the patient's autonomy. Choice D may exacerbate the patient's distress and compromise their well-being.

12. C: Choice C is the correct answer, as the client should begin to void and stop their stream before obtaining a clean catch urine sample directly into a sample cup. An additional method of collecting a clean catch urine sample could also be to have the client begin to urinate, stop, and place a new disposable graduated collection pan inside of the toilet to collect the remaining urine for sampling. Choice A is not the correct choice. It is not specified whether the sample included the initial stream of urine, and it also does not specify a method used to collect the specimen (i.e., the collection pan). Choices B and D are incorrect because it is recommended to purge the first stream of urine before collecting the sample.

13. C: Choice C is the correct answer, as in the face of obsessive-compulsive behavior, it's important to maintain a calm environment and gently redirect the patient when possible. Reporting the behavior to the nurse is crucial for initiating appropriate mental health interventions. Choices A, B, and D do not appropriately address the patient's needs and might either exacerbate their distress or delay necessary professional intervention.

14. C: Choice C is most appropriate because it provides encouragement but also acknowledges and validates the client's concerns and feelings. Choice A is not the most appropriate answer because this statement is dismissive of the client's feelings and may be providing a false promise. Choice B is not the most appropriate choice because this invalidates the client's feelings. Choice D is not the correct answer because clients should not be compared to other clients.

15. D: Choice D is correct because the CNA did not enter or exit the client's room, and they did not come into contact with the client. Choices A, B, and C are incorrect because these scenarios represent situations that require the CNA to perform hand hygiene.

16. A: Choice A is the correct answer, as the most appropriate response by the CNA would be to communicate with a colleague and assist the client to ambulate to the bathroom, as requested. This action promotes autonomy, dignity, and respect for the client. Choice B is incorrect because it would be inappropriate to put a client on the bedpan for convenience purposes. Choice C also is incorrect because it

would be inappropriate for the CNA to allow or encourage the client to be incontinent when they are capable of ambulating to the restroom. Choice D is not the most appropriate choice as the CNA was the caregiver asked to assist the client with their request.

17. B: Choice B is the correct answer, as the individual performing chest compressions should ideally be rotated out *at least every two minutes* to promote high-quality chest compressions and avoid caregiver fatigue. Choices A, C, and D are incorrect. It is not required to rotate out every thirty seconds, and it is not advisable to rotate out greater than every two minutes.

18. D: Choice D is the correct answer, as closed-loop communication involves receiving information from a sender and then following up with confirmation that the information was received. In this scenario, closed-loop communication looks like the client making a request, the CNA acknowledging the request and recognizing it is beyond their scope, notifying the nurse, and then closing the loop by providing a follow-up statement to the client. Choice A is incorrect because this is an open-ended statement. Choice B is vague and does not provide information to the client regarding how their request will be fulfilled. Choice C is incorrect because this statement does not acknowledge that the CNA can seek the assistance of a nurse to complete the client's request.

19. D: Choice D is the correct answer. While it's crucial to respect the spiritual and cultural needs of the patient and their family, the CNA must also consider the needs and rights of other patients. Discussing the situation with the supervisor allows the facility to look for a solution that respects both the patient's spiritual needs and the facility's policies. Choices A and B could either disrupt the comfort of other patients or disregard the spiritual needs of the patient and their family. Choice C could be seen as dismissive or unsympathetic to the family's request.

20. D: Choice D is the correct answer, as it is the only answer choice that addresses *both* privacy and comfort with exposing and cleaning one area at a time. Exposing one area to clean at a time keeps most of the body covered, and it also reduces the likelihood of the client getting too cold during the bath. Choices A and B are not the correct choices because they address client comfort only. Choice C is not the correct choice because it addresses only privacy.

21. D: Choice D is the correct answer, as setting the client's room up in a predictable, consistent way can allow the client to interact with their environment more freely and can promote the enhancement of self-care abilities. Choices A, B, and C are not the correct answers; these are interventions that would be useful for someone who is mildly to moderately visually impaired; however, these interventions would be relatively ineffective for someone who is blind.

22. D: Choice D is the correct answer. There are approximately 30 mL in 1 ounce. The client consumed 20 total ounces of liquids. Therefore, if there are 30 mL per 1 ounce, and the client consumed 20 total ounces of liquids, the client's total liquid intake would be 600 mL Choices A, B, and C are incorrect.

23. A: Choice A is the correct answer, as *NPO* means that the client may have *nothing by mouth* and would be unable to consume any food or beverage. Choice A is incorrect as this is a mechanical soft, thickened liquid diet that is appropriate for a client who has difficulty swallowing. Choice C is incorrect because this would be a liquid diet. Choice D is incorrect because this is a regular diet.

24. A: Choice A is the correct answer, as the most appropriate stress relieving practice the CNA can provide for the patient is to provide empathy through active listening. Choice B is inappropriate because the CNA should not educate on the detailed steps of the surgical procedure, as this is both inappropriate for the CNA to perform and not an appropriate stress reliever in this situation. Choices C and D are both effective long-term strategies, but they may not provide immediate relief in the short time frame leading

up to the surgery and are also typically handled by multiple different aspects of the medical team (for example: medical social workers)

25. C: Choice C is the correct answer, as the CNA would question the family's request for a heating pad because diabetes can involve a reduction in sensation due to neuropathy. This could lead to injury from a heating pad. Choices A, B, and D are not correct because the CNA would not question these requests.

26. A: Choice A is the correct answer, as assistive devices are anything that can be used by a client to assist them in completing care tasks and the activities of daily living. Examples can include walkers, prostheses, hearing aids, glasses, modified utensils, and many others. Choice B is not the best definition. Although assistive devices can help caregivers care for clients, assistive devices are client-centered. Choice C is not the correct answer because healthcare organization monitoring tools do not generally assist clients with performing independent care tasks. Choice D is not the most appropriate answer because although public resources (i.e., ramps and elevators) are considered assistive devices, they represent just one type of assistive device.

27. B: Choice B is the most appropriate answer choice because this client is reported to be bedridden. Passive range of motion movements are performed by the caregiver for clients who are unable to move their joints themselves. Choices A, C, and D are not the most appropriate answers because these clients are not reported to be immobile.

28. A: Choice A is the correct answer, as the promotion of blood *circulation* is the primary reason that turning a client who cannot reposition themselves is so critical. Lying in one position for more than two hours can lead to tissue death in areas where there is increased pressure (i.e., bony areas, pressure points). Choices B, C, and D are not correct because these are not the most important reasons for turning clients.

29. C: Choice C is the correct answer. When a patient dismisses a therapeutic activity as "childish" or "pointless," it's important to validate their feelings while explaining the potential benefits of the activity. Encourage the patient to try the activity and reassure them that they can stop at any time. This can help them feel more comfortable and respected. Choices A, B, and D either disregard the patient's feelings, undermine the therapeutic value of the activity, or may not adequately address the patient's needs.

30. C: Choice C is the correct answer, as a "code blue" announcement would indicate that there is a medical emergency. The CNA is *most likely* to assist with cardiopulmonary resuscitation (CPR) in this situation. Choices A, B, and D would not be the correct answer as these situations are not commonly associated with a "code blue."

31. C: Choice C is the correct answer, as speaking clearly and avoiding speaking too quickly is the most appropriate answer for increasing client comprehension. Choice A is not correct because speaking loudly or shouting can distort the sound and decrease the client's comprehension. Choice B is incorrect because standing five feet away could make hearing and seeing the speaker's face more difficult. Choice D is not the best choice because the television should be *turned off* to remove background noise and visual distractions.

32. B: Choice B is the correct answer, as the CNA can contribute to quality improvement by providing valuable insights and suggestions based on their direct interactions with patients and care processes. Choices A, C, and D are all beyond the scope of practice for the CNA.

33. A: Choice A is the correct answer, as it is recommended to wait thirty minutes after consumption of food or beverage before obtaining an oral temperature to avoid inaccurate results. The client's age, the temperature of the environment, and the client's health status can have an impact on a client's

temperature, not the *accuracy* of temperature measurement, making Choice B, Choice C, and Choice D incorrect.

34. D: Choice D is the correct answer. While it's important to provide reassurance and support, the patient's high level of anxiety may need professional intervention. Reporting to the supervising nurse is the best approach. Choices A and C oversimplify the patient's anxiety and may not be helpful. Choice B could lead to misinformation and is not the responsibility of the CNA.

35. C: Choice C is the correct answer, as patients have the right to access their medical records, which facilitates transparency and respects their autonomy. Choice A denies the patient's right to access their own records. Choice B imposes inappropriate financial barriers that hinder the patient's rights. Choice D incorrectly states that patients do not have the right to access their own medical records.

36. B: Choice B is the correct answer, as the most appropriate response is to address the client's complaint of pain since it is a factor in the client being resistant to ambulation. Giving time for pain relief can increase the likelihood of client compliance. Choice A is incorrect because this statement is less compassionate and does not address the client's complaint of pain. Choices C and D are also incorrect because they do not address the client's pain concern.

37. C: Choice C is the correct answer, as it's important to understand and respect professional boundaries as a CNA. Assisting with legal matters, such as a will, is beyond the scope of practice. The best response is to politely explain the issue to the patient and recommend they speak with a qualified professional, like a social worker or attorney. Choices A, B, and D either cross professional boundaries, neglect the patient's needs, or breach patient confidentiality.

38. A: Choice A is the correct answer, as providing a quiet, peaceful space where the patient can meditate respects their religious beliefs and supports their pain management strategy. It's important to recognize and respect the diverse ways in which patients cope with pain. Choices B, C, and D are incorrect, as they either disregard the patient's spiritual needs or attempt to impose alternative coping strategies on the patient.

39. B: Choice D is the correct answer, as the CNA role in care team meetings is to share observations and insights about the patients' conditions and responses to care. The CNA's direct interactions with patients provide valuable information that can contribute to the care planning process. Choice A undermines the collaborative approach, Choice C is beyond the scope of a CNA, and Choice D does not use the CNA's firsthand knowledge.

40. B: Choice B is the correct answer, as the appropriate action is to ask the CNA to slow down and provide more detailed information about each patient. This ensures proper shift handover communication and provides the CNA with the necessary information to provide appropriate care. Choice A may lead to gaps in care, Choice C is unproductive, and Choice D may not provide all the relevant information.

41. A: Choice A is the correct answer, as the most appropriate next step is to *call for help immediately*. Choice B is incorrect because the CNA should stop what they are doing if it is safe to do so, and they should immediately call for help without leaving the client unattended. Choice C is incorrect because it would be unsafe to leave the client alone to leave and notify the nurse. Calling for help is the safe choice. Choice D is incorrect because it is most important to call for immediate help while remaining with the client to ensure safety.

42. D: Choice D is the correct answer, as it is crucial for healthcare providers, including CNAs, to create an environment where patients feel comfortable expressing their concerns and have the assurance that their grievances will be heard and addressed. Choices A, B, and C are not directly related to the patient's concerns in this scenario.

43. B: Choice B is the correct answer, as the most appropriate action the CNA can take is to notify the nurse immediately to assess the wound prior to replacing the dressing. Choice A is not correct because the CNA should not replace the soiled dressing. Choice C is not correct because documentation would occur *after* notifying the nurse. Choice D is also not the most appropriate choice as the dressing change would ideally be completed after the nurse has assessed the wound.

44. C: Choice C is the correct answer, as yogurt is not a clear liquid. Jell-O, chicken broth, and popsicles are all examples of clear liquids, making Choice A, Choice B, and Choice D incorrect.

45. C: Choice C is the correct answer, as the gait belt should be applied around the client's waist, or the narrowest part of the torso. Choices A and B are incorrect because the gait belt should not be placed at the hips or under the breasts. Choice D is also incorrect because the client's waist does not always align with the belly button.

46. B: Choice B is the correct answer. In the given scenario, the role of the CNA is to document the patient's concerns accurately and communicate them to the appropriate healthcare professionals. By informing the charge nurse or the attending physician, the CNA ensures that the patient's concerns are brought to the attention of the responsible individuals who can address and involve the patient in the treatment decision-making process. Choice A is inappropriate and does not promote the patient's active involvement in the decision-making process surrounding their care. Choice C also exceeds the scope of practice for the CNA. Choice D does not directly address the patient's concerns about feeling excluded from decisions or support their right to be involved in the treatment choice.

47. C: Choice C is the correct answer, as the most appropriate first step to removing a shirt from a client with left-sided paralysis is by taking the unaffected arm from the shirt sleeve before lifting the collar of the shirt over the client's head and/or removing the affected arm from the shirt sleeve. Choices A, B, and D are incorrect because the first step should be to remove the unaffected arm from the shirt sleeve.

48. B: Choice B is the correct answer, as maintaining professional boundaries is crucial to ensure ethical and appropriate relationships with patients. Choice A blurs the line between professional and personal boundaries and may compromise objectivity. Choice C is discouraged and typically a breach of hospital policy. Choice D can compromise professional boundaries and may lead to inappropriate relationships.

49. D: Choice D is the correct answer, as the most appropriate response by the CNA would be to let the client know the nurse will be notified. Choice A is incorrect because this statement does not address the client's request. Choice B is incorrect because it is out of the CNA's scope of practice to adjust oxygen levels. Choice C is incorrect because it would not be appropriate for the CNA to suggest the client adjust their own oxygen level.

50. C: Choice C is the correct answer, as active listening involves fully focusing on and understanding the patient's words, emotions, and concerns. By acknowledging the patient's frustration and actively inviting them to share more about what is bothering them, the CNA shows genuine interest in understanding their perspective and feelings. Choices A and B, while they may be well-intentioned, do not demonstrate active listening. Choice D also does not directly address the patient's frustration or actively listen to their concerns.

51. A: Choice A is the correct answer because the presence of an indwelling urinary catheter puts a client at significant risk for a urinary tract infection (UTI). CNAs can help to reduce a client's risk of infection by ensuring regular perineal and catheter hygiene care. Choice B is incorrect because indwelling urinary catheters are more likely to contribute to the improvement of skin integrity rather than causing skin breakdown. Choice C is incorrect because urinary catheters do not increase the risk of dehydration. However, urinary catheters can assist caregivers with monitoring urinary output more closely, which can

assist in the prevention of dehydration. Lastly, Choice D is also incorrect because hemorrhage (a large amount of bleeding) can be a rare occurrence associated with rough placement of a catheter or trauma from pulling a catheter after placement. However, infection is the *most* significant risk factor associated with the presence of indwelling urinary catheters.

52. A: Choice A is the correct answer, as HIPAA (Health Insurance Portability and Accountability Act) is a federal law that safeguards the privacy and security of an individual's protected health information (PHI). It establishes standards for the electronic exchange of PHI and grants patients certain rights over their health information. The CNA's responsibility is to uphold patient privacy and confidentiality by adhering to HIPAA regulations. Choices B, C, and D do not accurately describe HIPAA nor the appropriate course of action for the CNA.

53. B: Choice B is the correct answer, as the posterior portion of the arm would be located at the client's *back*. Choice A is incorrect because the *front* of the arm would be the *anterior* arm. Choice C is incorrect because the *inside* portion of the arm would be the *medial* aspect of the arm. Choice D is also incorrect because the *outside* of the arm would be the *lateral* arm.

54. C: Choice C is the correct answer, as the tubing should be placed behind the client's ears after positioning the nasal prongs in the client's nostrils. Choice A is incorrect because this would be the step *after* placing the tubing behind the ears. Choice B is incorrect because securing with a strap around the head would be used with an oxygen mask, not a nasal cannula. Choice D is incorrect because allowing the tubing to fall in front of the client's chest would occur after the tubing is loosely secured at the neck.

55. A: Choice A is the correct answer, as appropriate use of hand hygiene is the single most effective means of preventing the spread of infection in the healthcare setting. Choices B, C, and D are incorrect. Even though these measures are important ways to prevent the spread of infection, they are not the *most effective* means of preventing the spread of infection.

56. B: Choice B is the correct answer, as the CNA should notify the nurse immediately in the event of a drastic change, such as new confusion or a new or changing symptom. Choices A, C, and D would not be the priority next step for this client. However, reorienting the client, calling a loved one, and offering a drink may be additional ways the CNA may be able to assist the client AFTER notifying the nurse.

57. C: Choice C is the correct answer. While CNAs are responsible for measuring and documenting vital signs, it is the role of a licensed healthcare professional, such as a nurse or physician, to interpret the significance of these measurements and make clinical decisions based on them. Choices A, B, and D are all within the scope of the CNA's responsibilities.

58. C: Choice C is the correct answer, as the wrists are at the LOWEST risk for skin breakdown related to immobility. The back of the head, sacrum, and heels are all at a high risk for skin breakdown related to immobility and pressure, making Choice A, Choice B, and Choice D incorrect.

59. D: Choice D is the correct answer, as comparing the client's armband to the client's verbalized identifiers is the *most* appropriate technique the CNA would use to confirm the client's identity. Choice A is not the most appropriate answer as transcribing the client's identifiers leaves more room for mistakes. Choice B is also not the most appropriate answer because the client is alert and oriented. Therefore, the safer choice is to have the client recite their identifiers while the CNA visually confirms what is on the armband. Choice C is not the most appropriate answer because it is significantly more reliable to have the client verbalize their own name and birthday rather than to have the caregiver read the identifiers aloud.

60. C: Choice C is the correct answer, as the patient's frequent tearfulness, expression of hopelessness, and lack of motivation to continue treatment are indicative of depressive symptoms. Choice A refers to a stage where individuals may initially struggle to accept or acknowledge their diagnosis or situation, often

avoiding or minimizing it. Choice *B* involves feelings of frustration, resentment, and a sense of unfairness. Choice *D* represents a stage where individuals come to terms with their situation and make peace with it.

Practice Test #3

1. The CNA is caring for a patient who is conscious and alert, but has difficulty swallowing due to a stroke. They insist on drinking water independently, but there's a risk of aspiration. What should the CNA do?
    a. Allow them to drink independently because it's their right.
    b. Forbid them from drinking independently due to the risk.
    c. Speak to the supervising nurse about the situation.
    d. Ignore the risk and allow them to drink to avoid confrontation.

2. The CNA is caring for a patient who has limited mobility and is at risk of pressure ulcers. They express hesitation and uncertainty about regular repositioning. How should the CNA handle this situation while respecting the principles of informed consent?
    a. Proceed with repositioning the patient, considering it a standard part of care to prevent pressure ulcers.
    b. Respect their concerns and refrain from repositioning them without their explicit informed consent.
    c. Engage in a thorough discussion with the patient, explaining the importance of repositioning and seeking their input in the decision-making process.
    d. Disregard the patient's hesitation and insist on repositioning them, emphasizing the potential negative consequences of not complying.

3. The CNA is caring for a patient who recently received a terminal diagnosis. The patient seems emotionally overwhelmed and asks for some alone time. What is the most appropriate response from the CNA?
    a. Stay with the patient to ensure they don't do anything drastic.
    b. Respect the patient's request but monitor them discreetly for safety.
    c. Inform the patient that it's better to talk about their feelings.
    d. Leave immediately and avoid the patient until they call for assistance.

4. The CNA is providing care for a client who has a history of stroke. Which of the following observations is most associated with stroke?
    a. The client has a pacemaker.
    b. The client is a fall risk.
    c. The client has weakness on one side.
    d. The client has a below-the-knee amputation.

5. A patient who recently had a stroke is now dealing with limited mobility and frequently expresses feelings of frustration and sadness. How should the CNA respond to the patient's emotional needs in this scenario?
    a. Encourage the patient to remain positive and not focus on their current limitations.
    b. Spend extra time talking with the patient and provide reassurance and empathy.
    c. Tell the patient that it's normal to feel frustrated and sad after such a major health event.
    d. Avoid discussing the patient's emotions and focus only on providing physical care.

6. Which of the following is LEAST likely to increase a client's fall risk?
   a. Incontinence
   b. Confusion
   c. Use of antibiotics
   d. Dehydration

7. After assisting the client to the bathroom, the CNA finds that the client is experiencing loose diarrhea with a very strong, foul odor. The client states that they are experiencing stomach pain. After assisting the client with using the bathroom and getting the client back to bed, the CNA notifies the client's nurse. Which of the following would the CNA NOT anticipate for this client?
   a. Airborne isolation precautions
   b. Decontamination of equipment using a bleach solution
   c. Hand hygiene with soap and water only
   d. An order for a stool sample

8. During a report, the CNA learns that a client has been confirmed to have a diagnosis of tuberculosis. Which of the following personal protective equipment worn by the caregiver is most associated with this infection?
   a. An N95 respirator
   b. A face shield
   c. Goggles
   d. A surgical mask

9. The CNA is assisting with maneuvering an elderly client in bed. Which skin injury does the CNA take care to avoid that can result from sliding the client?
   a. Pressure wound
   b. Skin tear
   c. Puncture
   d. Bruise

10. The CNA is caring for an elderly patient with advanced dementia. The patient often appears confused and has difficulty remembering the CNA's name. One day, they start referring to the CNA as their deceased spouse. What is the most appropriate course of action?
    a. Correct the patient each time and remind the patient of the CNA's name.
    b. Play along and respond to avoid upsetting the patient.
    c. Politely acknowledge the patient's error without correcting them and continue with assigned duties.
    d. Report the patient to the supervisor as someone who is disrespecting the CNA's role.

11. Which part of the CNA's body is primarily used to assist a client with standing during transfer?
    a. Legs
    b. Core
    c. Arms
    d. Chest

12. During dinner, the CNA sees that a client suddenly grasps their throat with eyes wide open. The client's face becomes red, and they appear to be unable to speak or make sounds. After calling for help, what is the most appropriate next action for the CNA to take?
    a. Check the client for a pulse.
    b. Perform abdominal thrusts from behind the client.
    c. Check the client's mouth for foreign objects.
    d. Begin chest compressions.

13. Which of the following attributes should a CNA develop to be able to effectively manage conflicts in a healthcare setting?
    a. Power dynamics
    b. Authoritative decision-making
    c. Emotional intelligence
    d. Avoidance strategies

14. The CNA notices that the care plan for a patient with advanced dementia doesn't reflect recent changes in the patient's behavior and health status. The CNA is aware that the healthcare team will be meeting soon for their routine meeting. In the context of team meetings in a healthcare setting, what is a key objective of discussing patient cases and collaborating on care decisions?
    a. To foster interdisciplinary collaboration and promote effective communication.
    b. To prioritize personal interests and assert individual authority in patient management.
    c. To allocate blame and responsibility for any lapses in patient care.
    d. To review administrative policies and procedures to ensure compliance.

15. The CNA is obtaining vital signs for a client. The client's temperature is 102.1 degrees Fahrenheit, pulse is 110, blood pressure is $\frac{130}{78}$, and respirations are 22. Which of the following is the most likely cause of the client's vital sign measurements?
    a. Heart attack
    b. Stroke
    c. Hypothermia
    d. Infection

16. The nurse has asked the CNA to measure orthostatic blood pressure for a client. Which of the following client positions would NOT be used for this procedure?
    a. Lying
    b. Side-lying
    c. Seated
    d. Standing

17. After washing a client's chest and stomach area during a bed bath, the CNA washes what area next?
    a. Face
    b. Arms
    c. Legs
    d. Back

18. The CNA is assisting the nurse with a dressing change. Upon completing the procedure, where is the MOST appropriate place for the CNA to dispose of the soiled wound dressing?
   a. The biohazard waste container
   b. The toilet
   c. The sharps container
   d. The trash can

19. The CNA cares for an immobile client. Which of the following complications is LEAST commonly associated with immobility?
   a. Wounds
   b. Pneumonia
   c. Diarrhea
   d. Contractures

20. The CNA is about to complete their shift and needs to provide a handoff report to the incoming CNA. Which of the following should be done in an effective handoff report?
   a. Share personal opinions about the patients to provide a holistic view of their condition.
   b. Focus only on the tasks completed during the shift without discussing patient conditions.
   c. Provide concise and accurate information about each patient's condition, care needs, and any changes.
   d. Omit any negative or challenging information to avoid complicating the handoff process.

21. The CNA enters a room to find that a client has fallen to the floor. Which of the following is the most appropriate next action for the CNA to take?
   a. Assist the client with getting back to bed.
   b. Roll the client to their side and notify the nurse.
   c. Call for help while remaining with the client.
   d. Check the client for breathing and pulse.

22. The CNA is assisting a client with dinner. The client uses supplemental oxygen via an oxygen tank and nasal cannula. The CNA can hear a faint hissing noise coming from the nasal cannula where it rests against the client's nose. Which of the following actions is most indicated in this situation?
   a. Continue to assist the client with dinner.
   b. Ask the client if they are in distress.
   c. Check the oxygen tank.
   d. Notify the nurse immediately.

23. A patient with a long history of bipolar disorder has started showing signs of mania, including increased energy, decreased need for sleep, and rapid, loud speech. What is the best course of action for the CNA in this situation?
   a. Engage the patient in calm, grounding activities and avoid participating in their high-energy behavior.
   b. Ignore the patient's manic behavior and hope that it will subside on its own over time.
   c. Try to counterbalance the patient's energy by encouraging them to participate in high-energy physical activities.
   d. Report the observed changes in the patient's behavior to the supervising nurse.

24. The CNA enters a client's room and finds them unresponsive to voice and touch. After calling for help, what is the most appropriate next step the CNA should take?
    a. Perform two rescue breaths.
    b. Begin chest compressions.
    c. Check for pulse and breathing.
    d. Tap the client's chest and yell, "Are you okay?"

25. What is the purpose of a gait belt?
    a. It stabilizes the client's core muscles during ambulation and transfer.
    b. It provides a way for caregivers to catch clients if they fall during ambulation and transfer.
    c. It provides a handle for clients to hold onto during ambulation and transfer.
    d. It allows caregivers to guide and stabilize clients during ambulation and transfer.

26. During a shift report, the CNA is notified that one of their assigned clients is on airborne isolation precautions. What does this mean?
    a. The client is infected with a pathogen that easily spreads longer distances through the air.
    b. The client is infected with a pathogen that is easily spread through touching contaminated surfaces.
    c. The client is infected with a pathogen that can be spread shorter distances when the client talks, sneezes, or coughs.
    d. The client is infected with a spore-like pathogen that can be spread by touch and requires decontamination with bleach.

27. The CNA is decontaminating a piece of equipment after it has been used for the care of a client with *C. difficile*. Which of the following products would be MOST appropriate for the CNA to choose?
    a. Soap and water
    b. Bleach product
    c. Disinfectant product
    d. Alcohol product

28. The CNA is assigned to care for a patient of Jewish faith who strictly observes the Sabbath, from Friday evening to Saturday evening. During this time, the use of electronic devices is prohibited according to their beliefs. What would be the best way to approach this as the CNA?
    a. Ensure that necessary care is delivered in a way that aligns with their religious practices.
    b. Inform the patient that medical care must take precedence over religious customs.
    c. Ask another staff member to care for the patient during the Sabbath.
    d. Ignore the patient's beliefs and continue using electronic devices as required.

29. Which of the following is an example of fine motor skills?
    a. Writing
    b. Throwing a ball
    c. Walking
    d. Sitting

30. The CNA is assisting a client back to bed. The client has an indwelling urinary catheter. From which location is it appropriate to hang the drainage bag?
    a. The side rail
    b. The head of the bed
    c. The bed frame
    d. The IV pole

31. How can the CNA BEST support a blind client during meals?
   a. Describe the location and description of items on the tray.
   b. Open packaging and containers.
   c. Feed the client in small bites.
   d. Standby in case the client asks for assistance.

32. A cognitively impaired patient seems to be refusing a bath out of fear. How should the CNA respond?
   a. Insist on the bath for their personal hygiene.
   b. Skip the bath entirely, respecting their refusal.
   c. Provide comfort and find alternate ways to keep the patient clean.
   d. Report them to the supervising nurse as uncooperative.

33. The CNA is performing perineal care for a client who experienced incontinence of stool. The CNA notes that the client's stool is black in color. The CNA knows to notify the nurse immediately. What can black stool indicate?
   a. Infection
   b. Bleeding
   c. Constipation
   d. Diarrhea

34. Which client position is typically recommended for passive range of motion exercises?
   a. Fowler's
   b. Sims'
   c. Prone
   d. Supine

35. During a routine check, the CNA notices that a patient's IV infusion pump is beeping loudly. What should the CNA do first?
   a. Turn off the alarm to stop the beeping.
   b. Notify the nurse immediately about the alarm.
   c. Check the patient's vital signs and document the beeping in the chart.
   d. Ignore the beeping and continue with routine tasks.

36. The CNA is exiting the room of a client on airborne and contact precautions. Which of the following items should the CNA remove first?
   a. Gloves
   b. Gown
   c. Mask
   d. Goggles

37. A patient expresses dissatisfaction with their current healthcare plan and requests the CNA's advice on alternative treatments they found online. How should the CNA respond?
   a. Share personal opinions and recommend alternative treatments.
   b. Dismiss the patient's concerns and reassure them that the current plan is best.
   c. Validate their concerns and suggest that they discuss their options with their healthcare provider.
   d. Tell the patient that their current healthcare plan will work better than any alternative treatment.

38. The CNA is working on night shift and encounters a disagreement with another CNA regarding the best approach for a patient's care. The unit manager is currently not available. What is the most effective way to resolve this conflict?
   a. Ignore the disagreement and continue providing patient care.
   b. Insist on personal perspective and confront the team member about their differing opinion.
   c. Seek a collaborative discussion to understand each other's viewpoints and find a mutually agreeable solution.
   d. Complain to the nurse about the team member's differing opinion.

39. The CNA would avoid using an electric razor with which of the following clients?
   a. A client with diabetes
   b. A client who uses supplemental oxygen
   c. A client who is receiving antibiotics
   d. A client who is on blood thinners

40. The CNA is preparing to enter a client's room to assist with toileting. The client is on airborne and contact precautions. The CNA must don gloves, a gown, a mask, and goggles. Which item does the CNA put on first?
   a. Gloves
   b. Gown
   c. Mask
   d. Goggles

41. The CNA is participating in a code. Which of the following factors is of the HIGHEST importance when performing cardiopulmonary resuscitation (CPR)?
   a. Early activation of the emergency response system
   b. Appropriate technique for rescue breaths
   c. High-quality chest compressions
   d. Presence of more than one caregiver

42. The CNA knows they would NOT trim which of the following client's nails?
   a. A client with hypothyroidism
   b. An unconscious client
   c. A client with a pressure wound
   d. A client with diabetes

43. A patient with dementia often becomes agitated and anxious during personal care routines such as bathing and dressing. As a CNA, what would be the best approach to address this issue?
   a. Rush through the care routine to minimize the time the patient spends in distress.
   b. Schedule care routines when the patient is typically in a better mood, even if it's not the usual time for such tasks.
   c. Ask the family members to perform these tasks, as the patient might feel more comfortable with them.
   d. Use a calm and reassuring approach during these routines and explain each step before doing it.

44. The CNA finishes assisting a client with perineal care. What is the most appropriate time for the CNA to dispose of their gloves?
    a. Just after exiting the client's room
    b. Just before exiting the client's room
    c. Any time before exiting the client's room
    d. Just after completing the perineal care

45. Which of the following is true when assisting clients with activities of daily living?
    a. Provide as much assistance as possible.
    b. Encourage clients to do as much as they can.
    c. Perform activities for the client if they refuse.
    d. Provide assistance only when requested by the client.

46. Two CNAs are assisting a client with moving up in bed. They know they should pull the client up in bed using what?
    a. The client's gown
    b. The fitted sheet
    c. The draw sheet
    d. The disposable pad

47. The nurse calls the CNA to get additional help and retrieve an AED for an unresponsive client. Upon returning with the AED, what is the first step the CNA should take?
    a. Place the pads on the client's chest.
    b. Follow the prompts on the device.
    c. Make sure no one is touching the client.
    d. Turn the device on.

48. A family member of a patient continuously interrupts the CNA's interactions with the patient and insists on being present during all care activities. What is the most appropriate action to take as the CNA?
    a. Allow the family member to remain present to keep them satisfied.
    b. Politely explain the need for privacy during certain care activities.
    c. Ignore the family member's requests and continue with assigned tasks.
    d. Request the family member to leave the room and inform the nurse about the situation.

49. A patient has a different cultural background and prefers to have a family member present during their care. Which of the following actions would be most appropriate to take as the CNA?
    a. Exclude the family member from the care setting to maintain professional boundaries.
    b. Allow the family member's participation with the patient's consent.
    c. Discourage the patient from involving family members in their care decisions.
    d. Seek legal permission before allowing the family member to participate.

50. While obtaining a client's vital signs, the CNA feels the client's pulse beat 45 times over 30 seconds. What does the CNA record for the client's pulse rate?
    a. 30
    b. 45
    c. 60
    d. 90

51. The CNA receives a report that a client is continent and can get up to the bathroom with caregiver assistance. Upon entering the client's room, the CNA finds that they are wearing a disposable incontinence brief. How should the CNA respond?
    a. Ask the client if they prefer a brief or to get up to the bathroom.
    b. Assist the client with replacing the brief if indicated.
    c. Make a note in the client's medical record.
    d. Notify the charge nurse.

52. What is the recommended depth the chest should be compressed to when performing chest compressions?
    a. 1 inch
    b. 1.5 inches
    c. 2 inches
    d. 3 inches

53. The CNA comes across a situation where a patient's family member has offered the CNA a monetary gift as a token of gratitude for the care provided. What should the CNA do?
    a. Accept the gift as their appreciation for the care provided.
    b. Politely decline the gift and explain that it is against policy to accept monetary gifts.
    c. Consult with other CNAs to decide whether or not to accept the gift.
    d. Accept the gift but inform the nurse or supervisor about the incident.

54. A patient from a South Asian background prefers to speak in their native language, which the CNA does not understand. They also follow specific dietary customs. What is the most appropriate action to take as the CNA?
    a. Use a translation service or find a staff member who speaks the patient's language to facilitate communication.
    b. Ask the patient to communicate in English for better understanding.
    c. Serve the patient the same food as everyone else and hope they will eat it.
    d. Ignore the communication and dietary issues and assume the patient will adapt to the facility's routines.

55. The CNA has developed a strong bond with an elderly patient who relies on the CNA for emotional support. One day, the patient confides in the CNA about experiencing physical abuse from a family member. The patient pleads with the CNA not to report the incident, fearing retaliation and a worsening of their situation. What is the ethical responsibility of the CNA in this scenario?
    a. Respect the patient's wishes and maintain confidentiality, believing that frequent presence and support alone can mitigate the situation over time.
    b. Inform the immediate supervisor or nurse about the patient's disclosure.
    c. Personally confront the family member accused of abuse, urging them to stop and change their behavior.
    d. Seek guidance from an independent ethics committee or professional organization, ensuring a fair and unbiased assessment of the situation while also protecting the patient's confidentiality.

56. A patient with a history of mental health issues has been demonstrating increased agitation and hostility toward staff when asked to perform basic activities of daily living. In this situation, when is it appropriate to use restraints?
    a. When the patient's behavior escalates to physical aggression, and all other de-escalation techniques have been exhausted.
    b. As a preventive measure to avoid potential harm, even without immediate physical aggression.
    c. Whenever the staff feels overwhelmed or threatened by the patient's behavior, regardless of the level of aggression.
    d. Restraints should never be used, as they can be psychologically harmful and violate the patient's rights.

57. With which of the following clients would the CNA prioritize frequent mouth care?
    a. A client who had surgery five days ago
    b. An unconscious clienti
    c. A diabetic client
    d. A client being treated for a urinary tract infection

58. The CNA is caring for a patient that has recently been showing signs of cognitive decline. Which of the following observations is NOT specifically associated with the onset of Alzheimer's disease?
    a. Memory loss, especially regarding recent events or newly acquired information
    b. Difficulty with problem-solving and planning
    c. Challenges with completing familiar tasks, such as cooking or getting dressed
    d. Increased appetite and weight gain

59. The CNA enters a patient's room to provide care and finds them unresponsive and without a pulse. What is the CNA's initial responsibility in this situation?
    a. Begin performing CPR (cardiopulmonary resuscitation) immediately.
    b. Notify the nurse or healthcare provider of the patient's condition.
    c. Retrieve the automated external defibrillator (AED) and follow its instructions.
    d. Call for a Code Blue and activate the emergency response system.

60. The CNA is assisting the nurse who is inserting a urinary catheter. The CNA is asked to don sterile gloves prior to beginning the procedure. To apply the first glove, the CNA uses which technique?
    a. Grasp the fingers of the glove with one hand while carefully sliding the other hand inside the glove.
    b. Slide one to two fingers underneath the folded cuff while carefully sliding the other hand into the glove.
    c. Slide one hand into the glove without touching the glove with the other hand.
    d. Pinch the outside surface of the folded cuff with one hand while sliding the other hand into the glove.

Answer Explanations #3

1. C: Choice C is the correct answer, as it's crucial to maintain the balance between respecting patient autonomy and ensuring their safety. Discussing with a nurse can lead to solutions that accommodate both. Choices A, B, and D lack this balanced approach.

2. C: Choice C is the correct answer, as informed consent is a fundamental principle in healthcare that emphasizes respecting patients' rights to make decisions about their care based on adequate information. In this scenario, it is important to engage in open communication and seek the patient's input. Choices A and D disregard the patient's autonomy and violate the principle of informed consent. Choice B shows respect for the patient's concerns, but it does not address the patient's need for repositioning.

3. B: Choice B is the correct answer, as it's crucial to respect a patient's request for space, but it's equally important to ensure their safety, especially when they are emotionally distressed. Monitoring them discreetly respects their request while maintaining their safety. Choices A and C may infringe upon the patient's desire for solitude, while Choice D may neglect the patient's emotional and safety needs.

4. C: Choice C is the correct answer, as one-sided weakness or paralysis is the answer choice that is most associated with a history of stroke. Choice A is incorrect because the presence of a pacemaker is more related to a history of heart conditions and not stroke. Choice B is incorrect because this is not *most* associated with stroke. Choice D is incorrect because below-the-knee amputation is not typically associated with a history of stroke.

5. B: Choice B is the correct answer, as spending extra time talking with the patient and providing empathy and reassurance can help support their emotional needs. It's important to be present and to listen, offering comfort and understanding. Choices A, C, and D can either trivialize the patient's feelings, ignore their emotional needs, or focus solely on physical care.

6. C: Choice C is the correct answer, as the use of antibiotics is not necessarily associated with an increased risk of falls. However, IV medications can present a risk of tangling and falling over tubing and equipment during ambulation. Additionally, many medications increase the risk of falls. Choice A is incorrect because incontinence can lead to injury as the client is ambulating. Choice B is incorrect because this may lead a client to be unable to follow safety instructions, which can result in falls. Choice D is incorrect because dehydration can result in low blood pressure, which can cause dizziness or weakness during ambulation.

7. A: Choice A is the correct answer, as the client in this scenario has symptoms that could indicate the presence of a *C. difficile (C. diff)* infection. *C. diff* is a common hospital-acquired infection that is spread through *contact* with contaminated fecal matter. Therefore, it would not be expected that the client would be placed in airborne isolation. Choices B, C, and D are not the correct answer because these are examples of expected interventions for a client suspected of possibly having *C. diff*.

8. A: Choice A is the correct answer, as the personal protective equipment (PPE) that is most specifically associated with tuberculosis would be an N95 respirator, which is a filtered face mask. Tuberculosis is an infection that is transmitted by droplets created during things like speaking, coughing, and sneezing. Choices B and C are not directly correlated with droplet precautions and would not be the correct answer. Choice D is incorrect because a surgical mask does not provide the caregiver with adequate protection

against airborne droplets. However, it is indicated to have the client wear a surgical face mask to reduce the spread of droplets.

9. B: Choice *B* is the correct answer, as elderly clients tend to have more fragile, thinner skin. For this reason, care must be taken to avoid skin tears while sliding them into the bed. Choice *A* is incorrect because pressure injuries result from prolonged pressure on bony areas of the body. Choice *C* is incorrect because a puncture wound results from sharp or blunt force trauma to the skin. Choice *D* is incorrect because a bruise occurs more from hitting the body against a hard surface or object.

10. C: Choice *C* is the correct answer. In this situation, it's important to be sensitive to the patient's confusion and memory problems. Acknowledging the patient's error without correcting them respects their dignity while allowing care to continue effectively. While the CNA should not play into their delusions (Choice *B*), correcting them each time (Choice *A*) may cause additional confusion and distress. Choice *D* is incorrect because it misinterprets the patient's dementia symptoms as intentional disrespect.

11. A: Choice *A* is correct because the safest way to assist with transfers is by bending at the knees and using the lower body to support the client as they stand. Choice *B* is not the best answer because the primary use of the core muscles (abdominals and back muscles) with the use of the legs can lead the CNA to injure themselves. Choices *C* and *D* are also incorrect because the arms and chest are not the primary muscle groups used to assist a client with standing during transfer.

12. B: Choice *B* is the correct answer, as the most appropriate action is to perform abdominal thrusts from behind the client. The client is performing the universal sign for choking. Choices *A* and *D* are incorrect because the client is alert in this scenario. Choice *C* is incorrect because it is most critical to attempt to dislodge foreign objects from the airway via abdominal thrusts.

13. C: Choice *C* is the correct answer, as emotional intelligence involves the ability to recognize, understand, and manage one's own emotions, as well as to empathize with and understand the emotions of others. It helps in fostering open communication, active listening, and developing constructive relationships, which are key components in resolving conflicts effectively. While an understanding of power dynamics can provide insights into how conflicts may arise, it is not the attribute that a CNA should specifically develop to effectively manage conflicts; therefore, Choice *A* is incorrect. Choices *B* and *D* may not be the most effective approaches to use in conflict management.

14. A: Choice *A* is the correct answer, as one of the key objectives of discussing patient cases and collaborating on care decisions during team meetings in a healthcare setting is to foster interdisciplinary collaboration and promote effective communication. Team meetings provide an opportunity for healthcare professionals from various disciplines to come together, share information, exchange perspectives, and collaborate on the best course of action for the patient's care. Choices *B*, *C*, and *D* do not accurately reflect the key objective of collaborating during team meetings.

15. D: Choice *D* is the correct answer, as the client has a fever, elevated pulse, and rapid breathing rate. This could indicate that the client has an infection. Choices *A* and *B* are incorrect because the fever would be less associated with heart attack or stroke. Choice *C* is incorrect because hypothermia would result in low body temperature, not a fever.

16. B: Choice *B* is the correct answer, as a side-lying position would not be included in orthostatic blood pressure measurement. Choices *A*, *C*, and *D* are not correct because an orthostatic blood pressure measurement determines the difference in blood pressure when a client is in lying, seated, and standing positions.

17. C: Choice *C* is the correct answer, as the client's legs should be washed after the chest and stomach area. Generally, a bed bath moves from head to toe and from least soiled to most soiled areas. Bed baths should begin with the face and neck area, followed by the arms. The chest and stomach come next, followed by the legs. Next, the feet are washed and then the back. The perineal area is washed last. Choice A is incorrect because the face is washed first. Choice B is incorrect because the arms are washed prior to the client's chest and stomach. Choice D is incorrect because the back is washed after the legs and feet.

18. A: Choice A is the correct answer, as the most appropriate place to dispose of soiled wound dressings would be a biohazard waste container, which is used to dispose of anything contaminated with bodily fluids. Choices B and D are incorrect because soiled wound dressings should never be placed in the toilet or the trash can. Choice C is not the best choice as the sharps container is used to dispose of sharps, syringes, and blood.

19. C: Choice C is the correct answer because immobility is more likely to cause constipation, not diarrhea. Choices A, B, and D are not correct because these all represent complications associated with immobility.

20. C: Choice C is the correct answer, as an effective handoff report should include essential information relevant to the patient's condition, care requirements, and any changes that occurred during the shift. Choice A is not necessary and may detract from the objective information needed for continuity of care. Choice B can lead to gaps in understanding. Choice D may hinder the incoming CNA's ability to provide appropriate care and address potential issues.

21. C: Choice C is the correct answer, as the most appropriate next action the CNA should take would be to call for help while remaining with the client. Choices A and B are not appropriate because the client should not be moved due to the risk of further injury. Choice D is not the most appropriate next action because calling for help is the most appropriate, and the scenario does not indicate that the client is non-responsive.

22. A: Choice A is the correct answer, as a faint hissing noise coming from the nasal cannula where it meets the client's nose indicates air is flowing from the oxygen tank to the client's lungs. Therefore, the CNA should continue to assist the client with eating dinner as this is normal. Choices B, C, and D are not indicated in this scenario as there is no reason to be concerned that the client is not receiving adequate oxygenation.

23. D: Choice D is the correct answer, as manic episodes are serious and can result in harmful behavior if not managed properly. Reporting such changes in behavior to the nurse is crucial to ensure appropriate intervention and management. Choices A, B, and C do not address the severity of the situation or might contribute to an escalation of the patient's symptoms.

24. C: Choice C is the correct answer, as the most appropriate next step is to check the client for breathing and a pulse. Choices A and B are incorrect because it is important to confirm breathing and pulse first before determining whether to initiate cardiopulmonary resuscitation (CPR). Choice D is also incorrect because it has already been determined that the client is unresponsive to voice and touch.

25. D: Choice D is the correct answer, as gait belts provide a way for caregivers to support, guide, and stabilize clients during ambulation and transfer. Choice A is not correct because the gait belt is not intended to provide core muscle support. Choice B is incorrect because gait belts should never be used to catch a client if they fall. Gait belts can, however, be used to gently re-align the client if they begin to lose balance. Choice C is incorrect because the gait belt is secured to the client's waist and would not be used by the client as a handle.

26. A: Choice A is the correct answer, as airborne isolation indicates that the client is infected with a pathogen that is spread by small molecules in the air. These particles can travel longer distances. Choice B is incorrect because this definition describes contact isolation precautions. Choice C is incorrect because

this definition describes droplet isolation precautions. Choice D is incorrect because this definition describes contact PLUS isolation precautions.

27. B: Choice B is the correct answer, as the most appropriate choice would be a bleach-containing product. Choice A is not the correct answer, because soap and water are not the most effective products to use for decontamination of equipment. However, soap and water is the preferred method for performing hand hygiene after caring for a client with *C. diff*. Choices C and D are not correct because *C. diff* is a spore that is not effectively neutralized by disinfectants or alcohol products.

28. A: Choice A is the correct answer, as providing care that respects and aligns with a patient's religious practices is fundamental to patient-centered care. In this scenario, acknowledging and accommodating the patient's observance of the Sabbath is crucial. Choices B, C, and D are incorrect as they either disregard the patient's beliefs, pass off care responsibility, or potentially impose personal beliefs on the patient.

29. A: Choice A is the correct answer, as writing is an example of a fine motor skill. Choices B, C, and D are incorrect because these are all examples of gross motor skills.

30. C: Choice C is the correct answer, as an immovable portion of the bed frame is the most appropriate place to put the urinary drainage bag. Choice A is incorrect because the side rail is movable and can potentially cause issues with the flow or integrity of the tubing and bag. It may also cause injury related to the pulling of the catheter. Additionally, urinary drainage bags should always remain below the level of the bladder to prevent urine backflow. Choice B is incorrect because the head of the bed would put the bag above the level of the bladder and could result in the pulling of the catheter when the head of the bed is repositioned. Choice D is also incorrect because the IV pole should only be used for intravenous products. Additionally, placement on the IV pole would put the drainage bag above the level of the bladder.

31. A: Choice A is the correct answer, as the best choice to provide support for a blind client during meals would be to describe the items and their location on the meal tray. Opening packaging and containers, Choice B, is not correct as this may not be indicated for all blind clients and may limit the client's ability to independently perform care tasks for themselves. Feeding is also not the best answer because not all blind clients will require feeding, making Choice C incorrect. Lastly, standing by does not actively provide support for the client and would not be the best answer choice, making Choice D incorrect.

32. C: Choice C is the correct answer. The role as a CNA involves both respecting patient rights and ensuring their cleanliness. Understanding their fears and finding alternate ways to keep them clean respects their autonomy and ensures their hygiene. Choices A, B, and D do not balance these needs effectively.

33. B: Choice B is the correct answer, as black stool can indicate the presence of blood in the gastrointestinal tract. Choices A, C, and D are not correct because black stool is not most associated with infection, constipation, or diarrhea.

34. D: Choice D is the correct answer, as the recommended position for performing passive range of motion exercises for a client is the supine position (lying face up in bed). During passive range of motion, the CNA is performing the joint movements without the client's assistance. Choice A would not be the best choice because Fowler's position (sitting) would make leg and hip range of motion more challenging. Choice B is not correct because Sims'' position (side-lying) limits the range of motion on the side lying against the surface of the bed. Choice C is not the best choice because a prone position (lying face down) could create breathing difficulties for the client and limit the forward range of motion movements.

35. B: Choice B is the correct answer, as the first action should be to notify the nurse immediately about the alarm. This ensures that the nurse, who is responsible for the patient's medical care, is made aware of

the situation promptly. Choice A dismisses the alarm, does not address the underlying issue, and should not be done by the CNA. Choice C may delay necessary intervention, and Choice D can compromise patient safety.

36. A: Choice A is the correct answer. When removing (doffing) personal protective equipment (PPE), the correct sequence is to remove the gloves first. Choice B is incorrect because the gown is removed second. Choice D is incorrect because the goggles are removed third. Finally, Choice C is incorrect because the mask would be removed last.

37. C: Choice C is the correct answer, as the best response is to listen empathetically, validate their concerns, and suggest they discuss their options with their healthcare provider. Choice A is inappropriate and outside the scope of a CNA, while Choices B and D do not address the patient's dissatisfaction.

38. C: Choice C is the correct answer, as conflict resolution in healthcare requires open communication and a willingness to understand different perspectives. Choice A can compromise patient care and hinder teamwork. Choice B is narrow-minded and can escalate the conflict. Choice D may not lead to a satisfactory resolution and can strain professional relationships.

39. B: Choice B is the correct answer, as the CNA should avoid the use of electric razors with a client who receives supplemental oxygen because of the risk of fire and injury. Choices A, C, and D are incorrect because an electric razor is typically seen as a SAFER choice for shaving, even with clients at increased risk for infection or bleeding (i.e., diabetic clients or those on blood thinners).

40. B: Choice B is the correct answer, as the CNA would don the gown first. Choice C is incorrect because the mask is applied second. Choice D is also incorrect because the goggles would be applied third. Lastly, Choice A is incorrect because gloves would be put on last.

41. C: Choice C is the correct answer, as the factor that is of the highest importance when performing cardiopulmonary resuscitation (CPR) is a focus on uninterrupted, high-quality chest compressions. Choices A, B, and D are not the correct answers because the quality of chest compressions has been found to have the greatest impact on client outcomes.

42. D: Choice D is the correct answer, as the CNA would not perform nail trimming for a client with diabetes due to the risk of infection and complicated wound healing. The CNA needs to check with the nurse before trimming any client's nails; however, Choices A, B, and C do not automatically limit the CNA from trimming the client's nails.

43. D: Choice D is the correct answer, as using a calm and reassuring approach during personal care routines can help soothe an anxious and agitated patient. Explaining each step before performing it gives the patient an understanding of what to expect, which can reduce anxiety. Choice A rushes the process, which may lead to discomfort or distress. Choice B relies on the patient's mood, which might not be predictable. Choice C isn't always feasible or appropriate.

44. D: Choice D is the correct answer, as the most appropriate timing for removing the soiled gloves would be immediately following the perineal care. The CNA should dispose of the gloves and perform hand hygiene before moving on to the next task. Choice A is incorrect because gloves should never leave the client's room. Choices B and C are incorrect because the gloves used for perineal care should be removed after the procedure is complete.

45. B: Choice B is correct, as the CNA should encourage clients to perform at a level that is appropriate and possible for the client. Choice A is incorrect because caregivers should promote client independence whenever possible by encouraging client participation. Choice C is incorrect because the CNA should not continue if a client refuses care. Choice D is also not the correct choice because care should be provided as ordered and as appropriate. Therefore, care is not only provided when requested by the client.

46. C: Choice C is the correct answer, as the most appropriate way to pull a client up in bed is by pulling the draw sheet. Choice A is incorrect because clothing items should never be used to pull a client up in bed. Choice B is also incorrect because fitted sheets are not used to pull clients up in bed. Lastly, Choice D is incorrect because disposable pads are not recommended for pulling a client up in bed due to their lack of durability.

47. D: Choice D is the correct answer, as the first step the CNA should take is to turn the device on. Choice A is not correct because the CNA should await instructions as provided by the device after powering it on. Choice B is incorrect because the device must be on for the CNA to receive further instructions. Choice C is incorrect because chest compressions should only be paused when the device provides instructions to do so.

48. B: Choice B is the correct answer, as the most appropriate action is to politely explain the need for privacy during certain care activities. This maintains patient dignity and ensures focused care provision. Choice A may compromise the patient's comfort, and Choice C disregards the family member's concerns. Choice D may be necessary if the family member becomes uncooperative, but it should not be the first action that the CNA takes.

49. B: Choice B is the correct answer, as this option respects the patient's right to involve their chosen family member in their care and supports patient-centered care. Choice A disregards the patient's preferences and rights. Choice C discourages patient involvement of family members without valid reasons. Choice D unnecessarily seeks legal permission instead of respecting the patient's decision-making capacity.

50. D: Choice D is the correct answer, as the CNA counts 45 heartbeats in 30 seconds, which means that the client's pulse rate would be 90 beats per minute (60 seconds). Choices A and C are incorrect as these numbers are not associated with the client's pulse rate. Choice B is incorrect because 45 is the number of beats in 30 seconds, not 60 seconds (1 minute).

51. D: Choice D is the correct answer, as the most appropriate response by the CNA is to notify the charge nurse of the discrepancy. It is not appropriate for a caregiver to place a disposable incontinence brief on a client who can ambulate to the bathroom. Choice A is incorrect. It is not appropriate to ask the client if they prefer to use a brief if they are physically capable of ambulating to the bathroom. Choice B is incorrect because the client should not continue wearing an incontinence brief. Choice C is incorrect because noting this in the client's medical record does not address the discrepancy.

52. C: Choice C is the correct answer, as the recommended depth of chest compression in an adult client is two inches. Choices A, B, and D are not the correct choices, since it is recommended that chest compressions be two inches in depth.

53. B: Choice B is the correct answer, as politely declining the gift demonstrates integrity, professionalism, and adherence to organizational policies. Choice A can create a conflict of interest and compromise professional boundaries. Choice C may not provide clear guidance on the ethical decision at hand. Choice D still breaches policy and ethical guidelines.

54. A: Choice A is the correct answer, as using a translation service or finding a staff member who speaks the patient's language can enhance communication and understanding. Similarly, acknowledging and accommodating the patient's dietary customs can contribute to their comfort and overall well-being. Choices B, C, and D are incorrect, as they either impose a language barrier, disregard the patient's cultural dietary practices, or fail to address the communication and dietary needs of the patient.

55. B: Choice B is the correct answer. The CNA's primary responsibility is to ensure the well-being and safety of the patients under their care. The patient has disclosed experiencing physical abuse, which is a serious matter that should not be ignored. It is important to note that healthcare professionals fall under mandatory reporting guidelines for elder abuse, and there are legal consequences for both the provider and the facility for failing to report. Choices A, C, and D do not reflect the ethical obligation of the CNA to take immediate action and report the suspected abuse.

56. A: Choice A is the correct answer, as restraints should only be used as a last resort when the patient's behavior escalates to physical aggression and all other de-escalation techniques have been exhausted. Placing restraints must be done under the direction and supervision of a nurse and according to the facility's policies and protocols. Additionally, the use of restraints requires an order from the physician. Choices B and C are not appropriate times to use restraints, and Choice D suggests that restraints should never be used, which is also incorrect.

57. B: Choice B is the correct answer, as unconscious clients require more frequent mouth care due to not taking in fluids or food by mouth. They also tend to breathe from their mouth. Both factors can increase the risk of tooth and gum disease from a buildup of bacteria. Mouth care is a priority for every client; however, Choices A, C, and D would not be the greatest priority for frequency of mouth care.

58. D: Choice D is the correct answer. While changes in eating patterns and weight loss can be observed in individuals with Alzheimer's disease, increased appetite and weight gain are not commonly recognized as early signs or symptoms of the condition. Choices A, B, and C are all commonly associated with the onset of Alzheimer's disease.

59. D: Choice D is the correct answer. When encountering a patient in cardiac arrest, the immediate responsibility of a CNA is to call for a Code Blue and activate the emergency response system. Code Blue is a hospital-specific emergency code that alerts the healthcare team to respond urgently to a patient in cardiac arrest. By initiating a Code Blue, the appropriate medical professionals, including nurses, doctors, and other specialized responders, can be quickly notified and summoned to the scene to provide advanced life support interventions, such as CPR, defibrillation, and administration of emergency medications. Choices A, B, and C are all important interventions, but activating the emergency response system should always be the immediate initial action.

60. D: Choice D is the correct answer, as the correct technique for applying the first sterile glove would be to carefully pinch the outside surface of the folded cuff of the glove while sliding the other hand into the glove. Choice A is incorrect because pinching the fingers of the glove with an ungloved hand would result in contamination of the glove. Choice B is incorrect because sliding one to two fingers underneath the folded cuff is the technique used to apply the second sterile glove. Choice C is incorrect. Attempting to slide the hand into the glove without the assistance of the other hand would be very difficult and would likely result in contamination of the glove.

Practice Test #4

1. The nurse aide may use a slide board to:
    a. reduce risk of injury when transferring clients.
    b. prevent clients for aspirating while eating.
    c. prevent injury while the client is bathing.
    d. assist clients who cannot dress on their own.

2. Contact precautions for a client require a face shield, gown, and gloves. When caring for this client, the nurse aide SHOULD:
    a. use eyeglasses instead of a face shield.
    b. remove all PPE after exiting the client's room.
    c. put on the gloves first, before donning a gown.
    d. practice hand hygiene after removing all PPE.

3. The administration of nutrients through a catheter inserted into a vein is called:
    a. NPO.
    b. parenteral nutrition.
    c. nasogastric tube feeding.
    d. IV hydration.

4. To ensure that an accurate blood pressure measurement is taken, the nurse aide SHOULD:
    a. ask the client to cross their legs at the knee.
    b. take 2 measurements 30 minutes apart.
    c. have the client remove tight-fitting clothing.
    d. use the appropriate size blood pressure cuff.

5. Which of the following findings for an adult client should the nurse aide IMMEDIATELY report to the nurse?
    a. An axillary temperature of 102.3°F (39°C)
    b. An oxygen saturation of 96%
    c. A heart rate of 72 beats per minute
    d. A weight of 309 pounds

6. Before trimming a client's nails, the toenails should be soaked in warm water for:
    a. 5 to 10 minutes.
    b. 10 to 15 minutes.
    c. 15 to 20 minutes.
    d. 20 to 25 minutes.

7. A client who is normally responsive does not answer any of the nurse aide's questions when they enter the room to collect vital signs. The nurse aide SHOULD:
    a. report the change in the client's status to the nurse.
    b. gently shake the client to see if they are awake.
    c. tell the client they will be punished if they do not respond to questions.
    d. come back at a later time to collect vital signs.

8. Which of the following is NOT within the role of the nurse aide when caring for a client on TPN?
   a. Providing oral hygiene
   b. Adjusting the rate of infusion
   c. Applying lip lubricant
   d. Reporting a client complaint of chest pain to the nurse

9. While shaping a cast, the nurse aide should NOT:
   a. use pillows to support the cast while it dries.
   b. use their fingertips to shape the cast.
   c. report rough cast edges to the nurse.
   d. elevate a casted arm or leg to reduce swelling.

10. A nurse aide has been asked to dress a client with an IV in a pullover garment. The nurse aide SHOULD:
    a. disconnect the IV tubing from the bag.
    b. keep the IV bag below the client.
    c. put the garment on the client's weak side first.
    d. tell the nurse that the client cannot be dressed.

11. A client drank 6 oz of coffee. This intake should be recorded as:
    a. 6 oz
    b. 60 mL
    c. 30 mL
    d. 180 mL

12. Which of the following is an example of ensuring electrical safety?
    a. Nailing cords to the floor
    b. Discarding cords that are damaged or frayed
    c. Covering table lamps with lampshades
    d. Turning the lights off when leaving a room

13. While taking vital signs, the nurse aide counts 8 client respirations in 30 seconds. The client's respiratory rate is:
    a. 4 breaths per minute.
    b. 8 breaths per minute.
    c. 16 breaths per minute.
    d. 32 breaths per minute.

14. Which vitamin promotes the absorption of calcium for healthy bone production?
    a. Vitamin A
    b. Vitamin D
    c. Vitamin E
    d. Vitamin K

15. Scrambled eggs and shredded meats are on which diet?
    a. Low sodium
    b. Clear liquids
    c. High fiber
    d. Mechanical soft

16. A client expresses sadness and loneliness about having to be on continuous tube feeds. The nurse aide SHOULD respond:
    a. "I'm sorry you are having a difficult time with the feedings."
    b. "We have other clients with feeding tubes. I will see if they want to talk to you."
    c. "If you get better soon then the tubes can come out."
    d. "Complaining will only make you feel worse."

17. A nurse aide enters a client's room and finds the client bleeding profusely from an injury on their arm. After putting on gloves, what should the nurse aide do NEXT?
    a. Direct the client to wash their injury in the sink
    b. Apply firm, direct pressure to the wound
    c. Elevate the client's arm above their head
    d. Remove any objects from the wound

18. When caring for a client who is deaf or hard of hearing, the nurse aide SHOULD:
    a. describe the layout of the room.
    b. use a sign language interpreter as needed.
    c. speak while facing away from the client.
    d. offer materials in multiple languages.

19. When brushing the teeth of an unconscious client, the nurse aide SHOULD:
    a. lay the client flat.
    b. force a toothbrush between the teeth.
    c. brush the back of the tongue aggressively.
    d. report any choking symptoms to the nurse.

20. Which method is best for taking a newborn's temperature?
    a. Tympanic
    b. Oral
    c. Rectal
    d. Axillary

21. When placing a client in a high-Fowler's position, the nurse aide SHOULD:
    a. raise the foot of the bed above the head of the bed.
    b. raise the head of the bed to 45 degrees.
    c. raise the head of the bed to 60 – 90 degrees.
    d. place the client on their side with the upper leg sharply flexed.

22. When taking a tympanic temperature, the thermometer should be placed:
    a. under the armpit.
    b. inside the ear.
    c. under the tongue.
    d. in the rectum.

23. When communicating with a client who speaks a different language, the nurse aide SHOULD:
    a. talk loudly.
    b. speak quickly.
    c. use medical terms and abbreviations.
    d. use gestures and pictures.

24. A stool sample that is black and tarry is called:
    a. hematuria.
    b. melena.
    c. hematemesis.
    d. hematochezia.

25. When caring for a client who is in rehabilitation after a stroke, the nurse aide SHOULD:
    a. encourage the client to actively participate in their care.
    b. perform all activities of daily living for the client.
    c. ask the client's family to participate in care.
    d. force the client to learn new skills so they can be independent.

26. Which health care team member tests hearing and prescribes hearing aids?
    a. Dentist
    b. Audiologist
    c. Dietician
    d. Home health aide

27. A client with a recent above-the-knee amputation of the right leg is reporting pain in their right foot. The client is experiencing what type of pain?
    a. Acute
    b. Chronic
    c. Phantom
    d. Radiating

28. While caring for a client, the nurse aide notes that the client is sleeping comfortably in bed. The client's heart rate is 87 bpm and regular. Her Foley catheter bag contains 150 mL of pink, cloudy urine. She has consumed 400 mL of water from their water mug. Which finding should the nurse aide report to the nurse IMMEDIATELY?
    a. Activity level
    b. Heart rate
    c. Color and consistency of urine
    d. Water intake

29. When interviewing a client using an interpreter, the nurse aide SHOULD address questions to the:
    a. client.
    b. interpreter.
    c. nurse.
    d. client's family.

30. Which of the following instructions should be provided to a client before they provide a stool sample?
    a. "Do not put toilet tissue into the specimen container."
    b. "It is okay if urine also collects in the container."
    c. "Use the specimen container to scoop the stool from the toilet water."
    d. "Staff will not be able to assist you during voiding."

31. If not visibly soiled or wet, how often, at a minimum, should linens be changed in a long-term care facility?
    a. Twice daily
    b. Once daily
    c. Once per week
    d. Once per month

32. A nurse aide collected the following amounts from a client's catheter bag:

Time	Output
7:00	210 mL
13:20	365 mL
19:00	295 mL

The client's total output for this time period should be recorded as:
    a. 760 mL
    b. 790 mL
    c. 860 mL
    d. 870 mL

33. Before having the client step on a scale to be weighed, the nurse aide SHOULD:
    a. set the scale to 0.
    b. wash the client's feet.
    c. have the client undress.
    d. weigh another person to calibrate the scale.

34. A client begins to have a seizure. What should the nurse aide do FIRST?
    a. Move furniture and sharp objects away from the client
    b. Leave the client to call 911
    c. Place the client on their back
    d. Put a tongue blade in the client's mouth

35. To brush hair that is matted or tangled, the nurse aide SHOULD:
    a. start brushing at the scalp.
    b. cut out all tangles.
    c. style the hair in a way the aide thinks is best.
    d. begin at the ends of the hair and work toward the scalp.

36. When transferring a client with left-sided weakness from the bed to a wheelchair, the nurse aide SHOULD:
    a. get the client out of bed on their right side.
    b. lift the client from behind.
    c. use a mechanical lift.
    d. position the transfer belt directly under the client's arms.

37. Which client position is the most common for a gynecological or pelvic exam?
    a. Sims
    b. Prone
    c. Fowler's
    d. Lithotomy

38. To promote the client's feeling of safety, the nurse aide SHOULD:
    a. speak sternly with clients who do not follow hospital policies.
    b. Use a gentle touch and soft voice while providing care.
    c. Always leave the door to the client's room open.
    d. Remove dangerous personal objects from the client's room.

39. Which of the following is a violation of the client's right to privacy?
    a. Knocking before entering the room
    b. Keeping the client's body covered with a towel during a bath
    c. Emptying the client's urine drainage bag while visitors are present
    d. Closing the curtain before applying a condom catheter

40. A nurse aide is changing the dressing on a client who had surgery 2 days ago. They notice the edges of the wound have pulled apart and the underlying tissue is exposed. This type of wound should be described as:
    a. eviscerated.
    b. infected.
    c. dehisced.
    d. healed.

41. To avoid the spread of infection while filling a water mug for a client, the nurse aide SHOULD:
    a. avoid letting the ice scoop touch the mug, lid, or straw.
    b. take the water cart into the client's room.
    c. keep the ice chest open when not in use.
    d. leave the lid off the water mug.

42. Sudden onset of weakness on one side of the body and face can be a sign of:
    a. cardiac arrest.
    b. a seizure.
    c. choking.
    d. a cerebrovascular accident.

43. Which of the following age and pediatric restraint combinations is NOT appropriate to use when collecting vital signs?
    a. A 1-month-old swaddled with one arm out of the blanket
    b. A 2-year-old sitting in a chair with the parent in the room
    c. A 4-year-old sitting back-to-chest in a parent's lap
    d. A 14-year-old sitting on an exam table with the parent present

44. Standing while bathing increases the client's risk of:
    a. bladder infections.
    b. pressure sores.
    c. falls.
    d. burns.

45. What is the compression-to-breath ratio for 1-person CPR on an adult?
    a. 30 compressions to 2 breaths
    b. 15 compressions to 2 breaths
    c. 30 compressions to 1 breath
    d. 15 compressions to 1 breath

46. Accidental urine leakage during exercise or coughing is known as:
    a. stress incontinence.
    b. urge incontinence.
    c. reflex incontinence.
    d. overflow incontinence.

47. A client is nervous about an upcoming procedure and begins to hyperventilate. How SHOULD the nurse aide attempt to help them?
    a. Give the client a glass of water
    b. Tell the client to take deep breaths
    c. Ask the client to identify the source of their anxiety
    d. Suggest the client leave the room until they have calmed down

48. When dealing with an angry client, the nurse aide SHOULD:
    a. be angry and aggressive.
    b. speak loudly to ensure that they are heard.
    c. remain calm and use a normal volume and tone of voice.
    d. be passive, withdrawn, and quiet.

49. Which of the following does NOT typically occur as clients age?
    a. Appetite increases
    b. Taste and smell senses dull
    c. Caloric needs lower
    d. Digestive juice secretion decreases

50. Which type of waste is NOT matched with its correct disposal container?
    a. Capillary tubes; sharps container
    b. Feces; toilet
    c. Gauze with small amount of blood; regular garbage can
    d. Linen heavily soiled by blood; dirty linen receptacle

51. A client with alopecia has:
    a. hair loss.
    b. an itchy rash.
    c. excessive sweating.
    d. body lice.

52. Which of the following is an example of IMPROPER food safety handling?
    a. Washing hands with soap and water before preparing food.
    b. Discarding cooked leftovers from the refrigerator after 4 days.
    c. Using soap to wash all fruits and vegetables.
    d. Keeping cold foods below 40°F (4.5°C)

53. When performing 2-rescuer CPR on an infant, chest compressions should be done using:
    a. the heel of the hand.
    b. the 2-thumb-encircling hands method.
    c. 2 fingers on the sternum.
    d. 2 hands on top of each other with fingers interlocked.

54. If a client weighs 10 kg, what is their weight in pounds?
    a. 4.5 lb
    b. 12.2 lb
    c. 20 lb
    d. 22 lb

55. Pressure ulcers:
    a. are staged according to depth of skin injury.
    b. do not occur over bony prominences.
    c. can occur as early as 8 hours after pressure onset.
    d. only occur in clients over the age of 65.

56. A client shows signs of anaphylaxis while the nurse aide is assisting them with lunch. What should the nurse aide do FIRST?
    a. Induce vomiting
    b. Obtain the client's vital signs
    c. Notify the nurse
    d. Begin rescue breathing and chest compressions

57. Which of the following medical providers CANNOT prescribe medications?
    a. Physician assistant
    b. Nurse practitioner
    c. Physician
    d. Occupational therapist

58. A client with a terminal diagnosis appears tearful and upset. They share with the nurse aide their fears about their diagnosis. Which of the following is the BEST response by the nurse aide?
    a. "I promise the cancer will go away with the radiation treatments."
    b. "I had a friend with the same cancer and she's fine."
    c. "I know how you feel."
    d. "Thank you for sharing your feelings with me. I am sorry you are going through this."

59. A family member wants to visit a client on contact precautions and asks the nurse aide if they need a gown. How SHOULD the nurse aide respond?
    a. "Go on in. The gowns are only for the staff to wear."
    b. "If you will be here for more than 30 minutes, you will need to wear this gown."
    c. "Please wear the gown. It is our policy to protect you, your family, and others."
    d. "You have to wear the gown or security will escort you outside immediately."

60. A client ate 6 of the 8 carrots on their plate. What is their food intake percentage?
    a. 50%
    b. 60%
    c. 66%
    d. 75%

Answer Explanations #4

1. A: Slide boards are used to protect the safety of clients and nurse aides while transferring clients.

2. D: The nurse aide should always wash their hands after removing PPE.

3. B: Parenteral nutrition is the administration of nutrients through an IV catheter in a vein instead of the GI tract. It is used when the GI tract cannot be used.

4. D: Using the wrong size blood pressure cuff can provide an inaccurate reading.

5. A: A fever (a temperature higher than 100.4°F, or 38 °C) should be immediately reported to the nurse.

6. C: Toenails should be soaked for 15 to 20 minutes.

7. A: Any changes in responsiveness or mental status should be reported to the nurse.

8. B: Any adjustments to the rate, placement, or administration of TPN must be done by the nurse. Treat TPN similarly to any IV therapy.

9. B: Shape and support a wet cast with palms (NOT fingertips). Fingertips can cause dents in the cast that can lead to pressure sores.

10. C: When dressing a client, apply the garment to the weak arm first.

11. D: All I&Os should be recorded in milliliters. To convert to metric measurements, multiply by the appropriate conversion factor (in this case, $1\ oz = 30\ mL$).

$$\frac{6\ ml}{1\ oz} \times \frac{30\ ml}{1\ oz} = \mathbf{180\ mL}$$

12. B: Discarding worn electrical cords is a precaution for ensuring electrical safety.

13. C: Respiratory rate is breaths per minute. If the nurse aide counts 8 breaths in 30 seconds, the rate should be recorded as 16 breaths per minute.

14. B: Vitamin D promotes the absorption and metabolism of calcium (and phosphorous). It is necessary for healthy bone development.

15. D: Soft, semisolid, easily digestible foods such as scrambled eggs and shredded meats are found on a mechanical soft diet.

16. A: The nurse aide should listen to the client's concerns and provide emotional support.

17. B: The nurse aide should attempt to slow the bleeding by applying pressure to the wound.

18. B: Use a sign language interpreter when needed for clients who are deaf or hard of hearing.

19. D: Report choking symptoms, signs of pain, bleeding, or coughing to the nurse.

20. C: A rectal temperature is taken in infants and children under 3 years old to ensure an accurate measurement.

21. C: The head of the bed is raised to between 60 and 90 degrees in high-Fowler's position, 45 in Fowler's, and 30 in semi-Fowler's. Choice D is a description of Sims' position.

22. B: A tympanic temperature is taken by placing the thermometer in the client's ear.

23. D: It can be helpful to use gestures and pictures when communicating with clients speaking another language.

24. B: Melena is black or tarry stool, which results from bleeding in the stomach or upper GI tract. It should be reported to the nurse immediately.

25. A: The nurse aide's role in client rehabilitation is to promote the client's independence. The nurse aide should encourage the client to participate in their rehabilitation as they are able.

26. B: An audiologist tests hearing and prescribes hearing aids.

27. C: Phantom pain is felt in a body part that has been amputated.

28. C: The pink, cloudy urine should be reported to the nurse immediately. It can be a sign of an infection or other disorder.

29. A: When using an interpreter, the nurse aide should address the client.

30. A: Toilet tissue should not be placed into a stool specimen container but instead into a separate trash receptacle or the toilet.

31. C: Linen should be changed once or twice a week in long-term care or a client's home.

32. D: Add the three volumes to find the total volume:

$$210\,mL + 365\,mL + 295\,mL = \mathbf{870\,mL}$$

33. A: To take an accurate weight, set the scale to 0 before the client steps on the scale.

34. A: The client's safety is the most important concern when they are having a seizure. Move furniture and sharp objects away from the client to prevent injury.

35. D: Begin at the ends of the hair and work toward the scalp to brush tangled or matted hair. This helps ensure client comfort.

36. A: Get the client out of bed on their strong side and use the strong side first for transferring.

37. D: In a lithotomy position, the client is on their back with their feet in stirrups. This is a common position for a pelvic exam or vaginal birth.

38. B: Using a gentle touch and speaking in a soft voice are techniques that promote the client's feelings of safety.

39. C: Emptying the client's urine bag before visitors arrive respects the client's right to privacy.

40. C: Dehiscence occurs when the wound layers pull apart or separate. Clients may say they felt the wound "pop" open.

41. A: Avoid letting the ice scoop touch the mug, lid, or straw to prevent the spread of microbes between the water mug and ice scoop.

42. D: A cerebrovascular accident, or stroke, can cause weakness to one side of the body and face.

43. B: For comfort and safety, toddlers should be positioned in a parent's lap in a bear hug or back-to-chest position.

44. C: Standing while bathing can increase the risk of falls and dizziness.

45. A: One-person CPR on an adult or a child uses 30 compressions followed by 2 breaths.

46. A: Stress incontinence is loss of urine during exercise or certain straining movements such as sneezing, laughing, or coughing.

47. B: The nurse aide can assist the client in changing their physiologic response by directing them to take deep breaths. This will help the client focus on the present moment and help to alleviate the panic.

48. C: When dealing with an angry client, the nurse aide should remain calm and use a moderate volume and tone of voice.

49. A: Appetite decreases in older clients.

50. D: Linen that is lightly soiled can go in the dirty linen receptacle. However, linen that is heavily soiled by blood should be placed in a biohazard bag.

51. A: Alopecia is a condition that causes excessive hair loss.

52. C: Do not use soap or detergent to wash fruits and vegetables; they should be rinsed with tap water.

53. B: During 2-rescuer CPR on an infant, the 2-thumbencircling hands method should be used.

54. D: Multiply the weight in pounds by the appropriate conversion factor ($1\ kg = 2.2\ lb$).

$$\frac{10\ lbs}{1\ kg} \times \frac{2.21\ lbs}{1\ kg} = 22\ lbs$$

55. A: Pressure ulcers are staged according to depth of skin injury. They can occur as early as 2 – 6 hours after onset of pressure. Major causes are pressure, friction, and shearing that cause skin breakdown. These ulcers can occur in clients of any age, not just those over 65.

56. C: The priority for the nurse aide is to notify the nurse.

57. D: Occupational therapists cannot prescribe medications.

58. D: The best response when talking with upset clients is to acknowledge their pain and their feelings, show gratitude for their openness, and offer support.

59. C: Politely tell visitors to wear the proper PPE to protect themselves, the client, and their family.

60. D: Divide the amount of food eaten by the original amount:

$$\frac{6}{8} = 0.75$$

Multiple by 100 to convert to a percent:

$$0.75\ x\ 100 = \mathbf{75\%}$$

ONLINE RESOURCES

Ascencia includes online resources with the purchase of this study guide to help you fully prepare for the exam.

Practice Tests

In addition to the four practice exams included in this book, we also offer three exams online. Since many exams today are computer based, practicing your test-taking skills on the computer is a great way to prepare.

Review Questions

Need more practice? Our review questions use a variety of formats to help you memorize key terms and concepts.

Flash Cards

Trivium's flash cards allow you to review important terms easily on your computer or smartphone.

Cheat Sheets

Review the core skills you need to master the exam with easy-to-read Cheat Sheets.

From Stress to Success

Watch "From Stress to Success," a brief but insightful YouTube video that offers the tips, tricks, and secrets experts use to score higher on the exam.

Reviews

Leave a review, send us helpful feedback, or sign up for Trivium promotions—including free books!

Access these materials by following the link or scanning the QR code:

ascenciatestprep.com/cna-online-resources